Best wishes to you from Ramona

Gatwick

Another Day in the Country

Stories and Photographs from the Heartland

PAT WICK

Magician's Ink

Another Day in the Country

Stories and Photographs from the Heartland
Pat Wick

Magician's Ink
P.O. Box 12
Ramona, KS 67475
www.californiasisters.com

Printed in the USA
Print Source Direct
Hillsboro, KS

Library of Congress Control Number: 2005925094
ISBN: 0-9706331-1-4

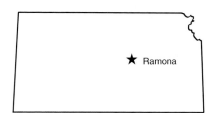

Cover photograph Pat Wick and Jessica Gilbert by Jill Cannefax

To Aaron Timothy Steinborn

who became our self-appointed guardian angel
enabling us to spend Another Day in the Country
with relative ease!

Our very own Tooltime Tim

The Cast of Characters: thank you for being our constant source of inspiration

Jana Wick

Naomi Ehrhardt Fike

OUR PARENTS
Laurel Ehrhardt & Martha Schubert Ehrhardt.

Anna Schubert Schimming

Frieda Schubert Struebing

Anton "Tony" Meyer

Erich Utech

Henry Hans Herman Schubert

Gertrude Hicks Schubert

Jessica Gilbert

Jake "Jakie" Brunner

Tim Steinborn

Emily Staatz

OUR GRANDPARENTS
Solomon Ehrhardt and Leah Glantz Ehrhardt / A. G. Schubert and Auguste Bentz Schubert

Introduction

Pat Wick
author/photographer

Ramona, Kansas, a tiny forgotten town in the middle of the prairie, has always been my heart's home. In a mobile, fast-paced world, Ramona was my one unchanging spot. My parents brought me here as a baby and we stayed until I was school age. Whether I was six or sixty, this place of my ancestors held a certain fascination.

My first memories of Ramona came from Strickler's store, owned by Uncle Vern. I can still see the bins of cookies in the display case. My greatest thrill was walking across the street, holding tight to Grandpa Ehrhardt's hand on a Saturday night, to get a chocolate ice cream cone at Georgia's Café.

Once I grew up, I returned to Ramona spasmodically—mostly for funerals. Each time I visited, I was more enchanted with the nostalgia of being here again where several generations of my ancestors had lived. And then in 1990, a dream of owning land in Ramona became reality, when I bought a dilapidated little old house on main street which my sister, Jessica, and I started to reclaim. That year I began to write the stories of the people in Ramona, stories that needed to be told to future generations, only dreaming they would ever be published. I began taking pictures to record the people in this town, the pastoral scenes and this experience of life in the country so that I would never forget the wonder of it all. I wanted my children to know Ramona—a rural American way of life that is fast becoming extinct. I wanted them to appreciate a wisdom beyond technology. I longed for them to experience a quiet place where they could discover and hear the cadence of nature.

In 1995 we bought a second house, calling it Cousin's Corner, so that our cousins would have a place to stay when they came to visit. In the year 2000 we made this huge leap and decided to move to Ramona. "At least for a year," I said. My stories started appearing in *The Marion County Record*, and the following year we opened Cousin's Corner Bed and Breakfast as a way of earning a living in the country. It's 2005 and we're still here!

You hold in your hands only half of the stories written and a fraction of the pictures I've taken. My camera keeps clicking and every week another story is born, sharing what it's like to spend another day in the country. It's my heart's desire that as you read, you, too, will be taken back to a more simple, gentle way of life. May this book be a touchstone to your own heart's home.

Patwick

The California Sisters, Jessica Gilbert and Pat Wick at Jacob's Crossing east of Ramona. Circa 2004

Shall We Dance?

This waltz between a writer and the reader is a little like tripping the light fantastic. I'm very aware that it takes two to tango. I'm feeling like a teenager at my first dance, wondering if anyone will actually invite me to get out on the floor and dance with them.

I'm wondering who is going to read my stories about Ramona, and I wonder will we become friends? Do I need to introduce myself before I ask you to be my partner?

Several years ago, I came to spend the summer in the country. It was quite a shift from what I had become accustomed to in California and I liked the change of pace.

I'm a writer so it was as natural as breathing to record this experience. Eventually I had several stories written, and I told my aunt Anna, who has lived most of her life on a farm between Ramona and Hope, "I'd like to do a newspaper column for the *Marion County Record.*"

"Ohhh," said my aunt as she raised her eyebrows and nodded her head, scrutinizing me and my resolve. "What would you write about, Patricia?" (My aunt calls everyone by their full name.)

"I'd write about the people," I said. "I've even got a name for the column—It's Just Another Day in the Country."

Several months later my aunt wrote me a note after I was back home in Napa Valley. "So, Patricia, have you talked to the editor of *The Marion County Record* about writing that column? When can we expect to see it?"

Would you believe it took me five years—until 2000 when I moved to Kansas—before I actually talked to Bill Meyer, editor of the newspaper? I discovered it was just too difficult to write about Kansas when I was living in California.

Country time definitely runs at a different pace. Ramona is a quiet town—a quiet so permeating that I can identify individual bird calls. In the city you hear a conglomeration of congested noise, but not here. There is no layering of sound in Ramona, where the population always hovers around 100.

On a quiet morning in summer you can hear a mockingbird sing, a screen door slam, the train go through, doves coo, clothes flap on the line, and a dog bark. These are all singular experiences.

There is a spacious quality about this prairie that my sister and I so enjoy. When we turn off Highway 77 and start down the gravel road toward Ramona we often open up the windows, and just breath in that country air.

It's amazing to see a complete circle of horizon with the blue-domed sky overhead. There's this feeling that "We're home!" It must be in our genetic coding.

Folks who live here all the time get used to these breath-taking scenes and perhaps take them for granted. But believe me, Kansas holds the record for beautiful sunsets! Even the ocean at sundown pales into insignificance against the grandeur of a prairie sunset with its cloud formations and infinite color combinations.

I love to watch the countryside rhythmically change colors with the seasons. The wheat fields go from green to gold, the black earth freshly tilled and fragrant, the blaze of yellow sunflowers, the russet of ripening milo, the silver fragility of corn stocks still standing as a windbreak in winter, and the white early morning frost on the bare black trees.

Through it all—like colors woven in a tapestry—are the people in my town. They are a stalwart, mostly older bunch of residents who have survived many a winter storm with a steady tread. I think of the color blue because they are true blue—clad in faded blue overalls or denim jackets with a feed cap pulled down to their eyebrows.

The color red stands for the new people who have arrived in town during the past few years—new blood. These folk are still feeling their way into leadership and wondering what kind of community it will become with this transfusion.

With the country as my palette, and nature as my inspiration, I paint pictures of the people, and the pulse of this small town on the prairie that has always been my heart's home.

So shall we dance? I'll write. Will you read? And together we'll celebrate the wonders of another day in the country?

Our grandfather, A. G. Schubert, was one of the founders of the original co-op in Ramona, KS. Circa 1992

Coming Home

The poet Maya Angelou once said that you can never leave the place of your birth. It is as firmly imbedded in your being as your genetic coding and it manifests itself all through your lifetime in the way you talk, the way you walk and even in the way you think.

Like the salmon that return to the mountain stream of their spawning, or the swallows to your barn, my sister and I were drawn to the tiny town in Kansas called Ramona, for it was in Ramona that our grandparents formed a union, farmed and lived. It was in Ramona that our parents were born, raised and schooled. Ramona holds our roots and we return again and again to pick up the strands of family ties and celebrate the family holidays in Ramona.

Ramona was born in 1887 and the town fathers had to show evidence of at least 250 residents in order to form the town. The downtown section of town—about a block long—was a thriving business community once.

They tell me my town even had a doctor's office with Doc Saylor in residence from 1905-1932. Ramona had a blacksmith shop, a tavern, a lumber yard, a cream station, Strickler's Mercantile—which sold everything from eggs to overalls—a post office, a grocery store, a bank, a hotel, a barber shop, a service station (after the advent of cars), an implement store and even a realty office.

Most of these buildings are long gone, only recalled in faded photographs. The lumberyard eventually closed and became a "pool hall," as my grandma used to say. It then became a succession of restaurants and an antique shop for awhile. The Mercantile burned down in 1955. The summer of 1995 Tatge's Garage fell down and the old Ramona Garage is threatening to do the same.

As is true in most small towns in Marion County, Kansas, there is no longer a school here. The grade school was torn down and those bricks went into the Stroda home west of town. The high school at the north end of town became the home of Tatge Manufacturing which makes The Wik, an insecticide-laced cow scratcher, and employs a few local people.

The summer of 2000, the town held its collective breath as Betty Ohm's restaurant and Hanschu's Market both closed. "Will Ramona disappear?" we wondered. "How can a town survive without a business district?" we asked.

We used to tell our friends in California about our experiences coming back to Kansas. We told them about the bank where you are known by your family reputation, about the fact that it is open only Tuesday morning for two hours and Friday afternoon for the same amount of time.

We told them about the Ramona Garage that was "open on demand," and you'd have to go to the cafe and find Maurice if you wanted gas. We told them about neighbors who come to your rescue at the drop of a hat and they had trouble believing our stories.

My father called from Oregon—his daughters going back to Kansas stirred up many memories for him. He reminded me that there used to be several churches in town when he was a boy. He remembers best a charismatic group on the corner of Fourth & B Streets (of course, streets didn't have names back then) where the teenagers in town loved to congregate outside the windows waiting for someone to get the spirit.

The Trinity Lutheran church is the only church in the city limits now. On Sunday mornings you can still hear the bell toll, ringing out across the still country air calling in the faithful.

As surely as the bell tolls reminding the members of their soul's salvation, our souls were drawn to return to Ramona. "I don't understand you girls," said my father, "I worked so hard to get out of town and here you are trying to go back."

My only reply is, "It's the circle of life." People go out and come back, winter turns to spring, the sun rises and sets and here I am enjoying another day in the country.

Missy, one of a zillion cats in town, raised her brood on our front porch. Circa 2002

Sunday Dinner

Sunday dinner at Grandma's house was an occasion that I rarely experienced, but I heard a lot of stories. My grandmother would cook a huge Sunday dinner for twenty or thirty people every week.

"Your grandma was always taking care of some relation," Uncle Hank tells me. "For instance our cousins lost their mother early on, so all of the their family would come for Sunday dinner to join us—right there that was twenty-some between our family and theirs."

For years Grandma did all this cooking on an old wood cook stove. She had no refrigerator in the beginning—there was just the well house with cool water running through the wood trough. Or there was the cellar, chilly and damp.

I can hardly fathom what it was like to be without running water, a garbage disposal, two ovens and a deep freeze.

After dinner, the men in the family would sit around swapping stories or playing cards. The women would retire to the kitchen to clean up the mess. Sometimes the girls would start to sing.

Someone in the family had a camera, because we have pictures of these family gatherings. The passage of time was marked by photographs of cousins and other relatives getting taller and older from one picture to another.

Even after you were married with a family of your own, it was the custom among our relatives to still attend Grandma's Sunday dinner. And if you weren't there, she'd ask where you were.

Eventually, the required attendance began to diminish. The children moved away to find jobs in far away places. My grandparents moved into town to a smaller house. Even so, at weddings and funerals, holidays and vacations, we found ourselves gathering around Grandma's table.

As these family events became more sparse, my aunts and uncles compensated for the weekly connection by carrying on the tradition of a yearly family dinner. Year after year they planned those chicken dinners and my sister and I rarely showed up. We were living on the West Coast and Kansas seemed a lifetime away. Then one year, that all changed.

Mom and Dad were celebrating their fiftieth wedding anniversary and they asked my sister and me to come back again with them to the family reunion in Ramona.

Over the Sunday dinner of fried chicken and cole slaw, we chatted with relatives. After dinner, I walked around Ramona with cousins that I hadn't seen in years. "There's something about this town that I just love," I confessed.

We walked down the familiar street, each of us absorbed in our own memories of childhood. Here was the park we played in, with the same set of swings and merry-go-round—familiar landmarks.

"It never changes," said our cousin, Gary, who grew up here.

"Let's check out Grandma's house," Cousin Alan suggested. "Do you think the people who own it would let us inside?"

Stan and Deb Wiles now owned Grandma's house and they graciously invited us in. "It's so small," one cousin said to another. "How did we all fit in this dining room?"

Awash in nostalgia, yesterday's children walked back to the Parish Hall to the remnants of Sunday dinner. The farm house that had held so many Sunday dinners was long gone. The house in town filled with fond memories was now owned by strangers. There was no longer a family dining room large enough to hold us all. We were like little birds without a familiar roost.

What was going to happen when we wanted to come back to Ramona in another ten years for reunion? Who, in our family, would still be here? Where would we go when we wanted to spend another day in the country?

This is the empty old house we found on Ramona's main street—after the weeds were cut down. Circa 1990

Land in Ramona

It was early in the morning on the day we were to fly back to California after a family reunion in Ramona. I was out walking the streets of town one last time. As I meandered I was remembering all the times I'd walked these streets before. As a child it was play—wandering, roaming, run-around play—with a pack of cousins.

"Who lives in these houses?" I wondered. "Are any of them empty?"

Turning down main street I spied a little neglected house behind a picket fence. No one lived there, I could tell. The lawn hadn't been mowed all summer. The place needed to be painted. The weeds at the back of the house were waist high. Windows were boarded shut.

Opening the gate, weak on its hinges, I walked down the sidewalk toward the front porch. There were concrete steps leading up to the porch and a wide veranda along two sides of the house. Porch boards creaked under my feet. One porch pillar sagged dangerously low on the north end, as if threatening to abandon ship. Everything leaned in that direction.

"Look at this porch," I said to myself, "It's beautiful." I was oblivious to the amount of work it was going to take to fix this place up. All I could see was my very own home in Ramona with the vision of uncles, aunts and cousins sitting on the porch visiting.

At the back of the house, stepping carefully to avoid holes and debris, I pushed open a rickety door that hung lopsided on one hinge. Climbing over stacks of boards, 2x4s, porch slats, and old windows that were stored inside, I looked around. There were hardwood floors in this house. I brushed aside spider webs and waded over more piles of lumber and found two small bedrooms, their windows broken and boarded up.

"Hello, little house," I said into the emptiness. "How would you like to belong to me?" Our family would have a gathering place in town. My kids would find a hub in Ramona, just as I had.

Closing the door behind me, I raced back to Aunt Naomi's where my aunt, parents, and sister were sitting down to breakfast.

"I've got something to show you," I said to my sister. "There's an empty house on main street."

"Are you girls packed?" my mother wanted to know.

"We've got to get going," my father said.

"We've got to make just one stop on the way out of town," I told them.

I led the way through the weeds up to the front porch. My sister and I climbed into the house, past the junk, over the boards, speaking in hushed excited tones. I pointed out the plaster walls, the hardwood floors, the original high ceilings, ignoring cracks, broken glass, and slanting floors.

My father honked the car horn, impatiently.

Back outside we circled gingerly around the old storm cellar, past the cistern, through the cedar trees, and came upon a flock of butterflies clinging to a tall weed stalk. "Aren't they beautiful?" my sister said.

"Do you know what they are called?" I asked her. "I think they're called California Sisters."

"It must be a sign," Jessica laughed. (For the dubious reader who's never seen a California Sister, and more knowledgeable about butterflies and their migratory patterns, they do exist; they look a little like a washed-out Admiral. In all honesty, though, I don't know that I've ever seen a California Sister in Kansas since—except for us, of course.) From that day forward, in my heart, that little house on the corner of Fifth and D was MY house. I never knew if I could actually ever own it. In fact, it took five years before I bought it.

If I'd had the gift of looking fifteen years into the future, I'm afraid I wouldn't have even believed that in the year 2001 I'd be sitting here in Ramona writing a column for you, reveling in the fact that I'm enjoying another day in the country.

We christened this The Ramona House, on the corner of Fifth and D Streets. Doesn't this legacy look lovely after we fixed her up? Circa 1995

The Legacy

"How much do you think it will cost me to fix up that house in Ramona?" I asked my father.

"Twenty thousand if it takes a dime," he answered. Where on earth would I get that kind of money for the frivolous whim of wanting land in my heartland?

"I don't care if the house has electricity," I said to my sister. "We can use kerosene lamps like Grandma did. We'll pretend we're camping." My own children looked askance.

For five years we returned to Ramona for events like the Centennial Celebration in 1987, and the annual Schubert family reunions. We'd walk past that little house with the picket fence and measure its decline.

Then one year, "Whoa, the picket fence is gone!" If we were going to do something it had to be quick. So in 1990 I made a bold move and got a signature loan for $5,000, and then bought the little white house in Ramona.

Early one summer morning in the cool Kansas dawn my sister and I stood on the sagging front porch of the little house, ready for work in our grubby old clothes and gloves several sizes too big.

"I have an Excedrin headache that's about 900 feet square," Jess announced, and we both started to laugh.

What were we doing here? It was only the second day of reclaiming our little dream house in Ramona and we were sore in every joint of our bodies. Our ten-day goal was a mighty big one for two city girls with a motley assortment of hand-me-down tools in a battered blue suitcase. But we were not alone! Once we committed to this venture the whole town seemed to kick in.

The generosity of the community was unparalleled. Mrs. Sader came down the street to offer us a cool glass of water, "I've got the best well in town," she said with pride. Nathan Bailey offered his garden hose since we didn't have running water. Jake Brunner brought cold Pepsi on hot afternoons. And David and Jane Staatz, from across the road, were there for any emergency. We soon called David, "Mr. 911."

"Traffic sure has picked up on the north end of town," said teenager Brenden Bailey. Indeed we were a novelty in this small Kansas town—two women, no men in sight, doing manual labor, and construction at that. On our tenth and final day we had the house repaired and dressed in a new coat of paint. She looked like a young Victorian maiden, with her porch the brim of an elegant bonnet. We called a town celebration and christened the house The Ramona House.

We may have had a house, but we had no electricity or plumbing in it, and we had no idea how this could be accomplished. Then a slim white envelop appeared in my California mailbox surprising us with the news that we had been given a legacy. Our Aunt Erna Schubert and her husband Dick Hensley had both died shortly before we came back and established the Ramona House. They had no children and unbeknownst to us they had bequeathed their estate to thirty-two nieces and nephews.

"Let's use it for The Ramona House," my sister and I said breathing a prayer of thanksgiving for this unexpected gift. Today beside the light switch in the living room you can see a picture of Aunt Erna and a plaque that reads, "Once more Aunt Erna lights up the room." In the bathroom there's another plaque that reads, "Thanks to Uncle Dick we're flush."

I don't know if my ancestors were concerned about leaving a legacy. But they did indeed leave one by the choices they made. Thankfully, their determined, strong, and good lives left a foundation that we now build upon.

Aunt Naomi kept our energy high with meals of mashed potatoes, fried chicken and cherry pie. Uncle Hank gave his tools and precious advice, often perching on the porch in the evening telling us stories of our ancestors.

"Come out and look in my storage sheds before you go buy something," said Aunt Gertie who is known as a "keeper" in the family.

Aunt Anna gave the couch that she wasn't using, and Aunt Frieda offered her car for us to use when we flew into Wichita for our ten-day visits. Cousin Keith gave a shelf he made in high school, his brother Gary, shared his expertise with gas furnaces, Cousin Janice helped paint and Cousin Becky brought her weed eater and helped clean the yard. The list goes on and on.

In the end, a legacy is just something of yourself that you share. Sometimes it's just so simple as giving yourself and your family another day in the country.

Downtown Ramona the year we moved to Kansas from California. The population hovers around a hundred people. Circa 2000

Small-Town Life

One hot summer afternoon about ten years ago, I do believe it was 105° in the shade with 99% humidity, Jakie Brunner pulled up in front of our Ramona House in his green 1957 Chevy, which he called his "fishing car." He fished two ice-cold cans of Pepsi out of his front seat and brought them into the house where we were scraping off old wallpaper and patching plaster.

"How did you know we liked Pepsi?" I asked our newfound friend. "Is it your favorite?"

"Naahh, sveethart," Jake said grinning. "I'm a Dr. Peppa man."

"So, how did you know?" my sister persisted.

"I just asked 'em down at the grocery store and they knew what you always bought," Jake continued, referring to Hanschu's Market.

Another neighbor from down the road, hearing this exchange, said, "You girls will soon learn that everybody in town knows every time you flush your toilet—and how much paper you used." That was our introduction to small town life.

Coming from California to a small town in Kansas, we were a little worried that we might break some "Code of the West" and embarrass our relatives. After all, we were only around for a few weeks in the summer, and our aunts and uncles were long-time residents. We knew that if we did something wrong, broke the social etiquette, they would sooner or later hear about it.

"You girls don't know what it's like," was a phrase our Aunt Gertie often uttered. She was right. We didn't know.

A small town does indeed teach you to be careful about what you say or do—at least it should! There is no such thing as anonymity in Ramona, where there are less than a hundred people in city limits. In such a little community you're known, your car is recognized, and neighbors quickly learn your habits. A reputation is hastily acquired and slow to be altered, so it better be good.

My cousin, Glenn, remembers the rigors of growing up in Ramona. "It could be hard—there were some who just loved to gossip and spread stories, and if you make a mistake as a teenager (which many often do), they'd never let you forget it! On the other hand, there were some wonderful people in town, who were so good to me. Did you ever know Bill Weber?" he asks. "He was the blacksmith in Ramona while I was growing up. He was a gruff, matter-of-fact kind of guy who always had time for me."

Glenn goes on with his list. "Wilbur Hanschu, he farmed near Ramona, and I went to high school with his brothers. I worked for Wilbur doing farm work, and that man always had something good to say about people." Wilbur was evidently the kind of man that you always felt free to talk to—even if you were a teenager.

"And what I regret most," my cousin continued, "is that I never told those guys how important they were to me when I was growing up."

It's another day in the country, and some things just never change.

They tell me this farmer's political statement comes out in the field every election year. Circa 2004

Culture Shock

"So how long did it take you to get used to being here?" Randy asked me the other day at the lumberyard. "To adjust, you know." He was measuring off some plastic for me to put on my north windows to keep the winter breeze out.

"Not too long," I assured him. I knew that he had family moving from the east coast to the Midwest and he wanted them to be happy here.

"How long before you felt like you fit in?" he continued the questioning.

"Ah, that!" I said and laughed, "I dunno—I may not ever; but we're happy. Funny thing is, now I go back to California and experience culture shock. Can't wait to get back to the country."

Fitting in? What does this mean? Perhaps if I fit in completely—as in not noticing anything different or unusual—there'd be nothing to write about.

Does fitting in mean that I belong here? Aunt Gertie always classified us as move-ins with an added advantage because our family roots were here, which theoretically made us "move-backs."

And what do I fit into? Not fancy clothes, that's for sure. I own one pair of nylons for dress-up occasions to go with the high heels pushed way back under the dresser and I haven't had either one on since my daughter got married. That's almost a year ago! Is that the way it is for all of you? Am I fitting in? I doubt it!

Last night my sister came back from Town Council and caught a glimpse of herself in the living room mirror. "Oh my word, I went to Town Council without make-up. I looked like a hick!" she was horrified. She'd been sick and bravely crawled out of bed to write her weekly newspaper column and attend the meeting—doing heroics. "What's become of us?" she lamented.

Perhaps fitting in has more to do with a mind set. I'm a Democrat in a largely Republican area, don't belong to the country club, the bowling league, Future Farmers of America, the co-op or a church. So where does that leave me?

We're beginning to know our way around. Just last week, I finally found a cleaners in Abilene. Several months ago we discovered a health food store in Salina. Today we tracked down a Calico Corners in Wichita so that we can find fabric to recover our couch.

Every once in awhile I have to call a halt, and remind myself why I'm in the country. It helps when our city friends visit and I walk the streets of Ramona with them and marvel once again at our local charm. That's when I know I'm really home—when I can smile at the charm and not balk at the inconvenience.

A month or so ago we brought a whole bunch of our stuff from California and discovered that some of it didn't fit in—the white leather couch strangely out of place, the wicker plant stands stored until next summer. If fitting in means everything from there fits here, it doesn't. If fitting in means being content with how things have always been—I'm not.

If fitting in is loving the land, exclaiming at the fall color, loving my leaky little house, appreciating the town folk and the slower pace, rejoicing that there is not traffic on the road, listening for the coyotes to howl at night, planting bulbs with dreams of spring grandeur, giving something back to the community—then, I'd say we're over the culture shock and ready to spend another day, another week, another year in the country!

Solomon and Leah Ehrhardt, our grandparents, lived on this farm west of Ramona until 1952. Circa 1995

The Sluice Gate

Isn't it something how life's circumstances alter the course of your existence like a giant sluice gate redirecting a vital stream of irrigation water from one field to another?

Everything is changed as one door closes and another opens. One field grows while another withers. One opportunity ripens for the picking and another dies on the vine. Ordinary experiences and every-day decisions can have repercussions that play on for generations. One such life-changing event happened to my family in Ramona during the 1920s.

Eleven of my grandfather's brothers and sisters—married with families of their own—decided to migrate to Lodi, California. Kansas was full of endless calamities with drought, dust, grasshoppers and hail. In California, they heard, you could grow grapes—not corn—and prosper.

"Why not take the chance?" they said to one another. "Why not?" So they sold their farms—five brothers and sisters going to the Promised Land. Their father, the patriarch—who had brought them here, bought and fought for this Kansas soil—was now dead. Their mother agreed to go along to yet another new country.

Each family member sold their land bequeathed to them by their father, and each family prepared for the move. They were going together on the train from Kansas to California with hope in their heart and endless optimism.

And then it happened—the sluice gate banged shut for one of the brothers—my grandfather, Solomon Ehrhardt.

The man who had purchased Solomon's land could not come up with the money. The farm was not sold and the family could not leave. They stood and waved goodbye to the others with heavy hearts still planted firmly, if unwillingly, on Kansas sod.

It is around this turnstile that my existence rests. They stayed, and because they stayed, my father—who was then a child—grew up in Ramona, met a young girl in Ramona, fell in love in Ramona, married and eventually lived near Ramona for a time when I was a small child. Through this turn of events, Ramona became home to me.

Seventy years have gone by since the fateful day Grandpa reclaimed the farm he didn't wish to have. And then one day his granddaughter, harboring fond memories of those farming days on the Kansas plains, returned to Ramona hunting for scraps of family history in order to piece together shards of her own life.

One evening I was looking through a neighbor's family pictures when I discovered a piece of my family's history.

"This was our old farm," our neighbor said as he showed me a picture. "In fact, I think at one time my father was going to buy your grandfather's land—I don't know what happened."

Later Aunt Naomi told me the story as we sat on her front porch. "His dad bought my dad's farm, and because of financial difficulty couldn't pay. So we stayed behind while the rest of the family went to California."

How amazing that my neighbor Leon's family turned out to be the keystone of my existence in Kansas!

One random dilemma to a Czechoslovakian immigrant, eking out an existence for his family in Kansas, changes the course of history for my entire family chain that immigrated from Germany. Without this circumstance my father would have grown up in California, far from Ramona. The middle Schubert daughter, destined to be my mother, would have married someone else.

For me it's just another day in the country, and I wonder in what way I may alter history today?

Erich Utech, one of our bachelor farmers, was our neighbor and his weekly load of laundry was my on-going photo opportunity. Circa 2001

Wash Day is Always Monday

It happens every week. I don't need a calendar to tell me what day it is—at the Sondergard home there's wash on the line — it's Monday!

Yes, I know, this is the day and age of automatic dryers; however on Fourth Street there are shirts and sheets flapping on the clothesline. I, too, enjoy hanging things out to dry in the Kansas breeze. There's just something about a line full of clothes that's fascinating.

"I get a lot of enjoyment out of being out there early in the morning all by myself daydreaming while I hang the clothes," says Darlene. "I wash on Mondays because it's traditional," she says with a chuckle.

Darlene hangs her laundry out the way my grandmother used to do it: Orderly! And she does this all year 'round. All the sheets with matching edges, followed by the pillowcases. All the shirts in a row with their relatives.

"When I do clothes I hang all of Kink's together, and then all of mine," she says, and she does graduated sizing as well. First the bath towels come marching past, then hand towels, and finally wash clothes bringing up the tail end as if they were playing *Crack the Whip* in the wind.

My grandmother arranged her clothes this way, too, and my mother taught me to do the same! Woe unto the one who hung things randomly.

My grandma Ehrhardt also had a strict sequence for washing clothes. Her separating technique took in more than lights and darks. First came white sheets and dish towels—the kind of thing that couldn't get heavily soiled. If you had a light load you could add white shirts to that mix but never underwear! Then came men's underwear—which got bleached to within an inch of their lives—then light clothes, dark clothes, and finally at the tail end came the work clothes, overalls and jeans.

There was good reasoning behind all of this because in those days Gramm was still washing with just *one* washing machine full of water, and two (sometimes three) tubs full of rinse water including the last tub that had bluing in it. (If by chance, someone younger than forty is reading this column they are probably going to wonder, "What the heck is bluing?") While we're at it, Grandma washed with one kind of soap—the kind she made herself out of fat and lye.

Now, the myriad brands of detergent, bleaches, laundry softeners, and enhancers boggle the mind. There's Tide, Gain, Dreft (oops is that one gone, too?), All, Cheer, Sun, Oxydol, Ivory Flakes, each made for special niches that are for cold water or warm. Grandma only used *hot* water! And she had the whitest clothes in town.

You've got to have a clothesline, straight and taunt to show off all the laundry. "I always washed my nicest things by hand," says my friend Paula, "and hung them on the line to dry—that is when I still *had* a line! Warren took my old one down and promised me a new one," she raises her eyebrows and is quiet for a moment. "The one we bought just didn't work right so we took it back and," she shrugs, "no line! I miss it!"

In every culture there's a clothes-drying technique. In Singapore, I was fascinated by a jillion long poles jutting out from high-rise apartment windows with laundry flapping from them—on Monday, of course! In Mexico, clothes hung on lines strung haphazardly between trees in faltering shade. In India, saris fluttered from second-story verandas like yards and yards of bright colored ribbon.

In every country I snapped pictures of laundry lines but none fascinate me quite so much as Kansas clotheslines. I even have a picture of my neighbor Erich's laundry—one complete ensemble hanging in a row: overalls, shirt, underwear, red handkerchief and socks—against a blue, blue sky.

My automatic dryer asks too many questions: How long? Permanent Press or Cotton? Air dry or heat? Give me a break! I'll just put these sheets out on the line and the wind will silently whip them so smooth you'll think they were ironed. And the smell is heavenly!

It's another day in the country, and you can just call me old-fashioned; I'll take a clothesline to a dryer any 'ole day!

Jessica stands by Grandpa Schubert's garage, the last of the buildings to go, on his farm west of town. Circa 1986

The Big Gamble

Almost all of us in this country are immigrants, giving thanks that our ancestors had the foresight to come to this great land. We daily reap the results of our ancestor's "big gamble" when they left everything they knew and traded it for opportunity and freedom.

Depending upon which wave of immigration your family boat sailed on, the reason for leaving the homeland varied. For those arriving from Ireland it was escaping poverty or famine. For those coming from Europe it was often avoiding a war they didn't believe in.

Whether it was from Czechoslovakia searching for opportunity, or from Germany yearning to own land, our ancestors came. English citizens came to escape religious persecution; others journeyed to escape social persecution. A friend's mother came at the age of seventeen from France to escape a bad marriage and the stigma of divorce.

This coming to America was a big risk, an important decision—maybe the most important of their lifetime—and it set the stage, and changed the course of each member of the family who was born thereafter.

When I came from the city to the heartland I was once again reminded of the continuity of family names in this area. I stood looking at the pictures of graduates from Centre High School the other day, and noted the generations and the names appearing and reappearing through the years—fathers, sons, daughters, cousins. Pictured there were my neighbors—in their youth—still living here, experiencing an interconnectedness that we take for granted.

My great-grandparents came from Germany to this country. We are an immigrated family with roots in Russia and Poland as well. My daughter's grandparents on her father's side were first generation immigrants from Norway—making the decision to leave, knowing full well they would probably never be able to return. They didn't.

After a generation or two the immigration often starts again—not to foreign lands but to strange cities and far off states. My parents didn't stay in Ramona, neither did my cousins—economics forced them away as surely as it moved our great-grandparents from Germany to Kansas in the first place.

The family farm just west of Ramona was sold fifty years ago, the family home leveled, the landmarks gone except for a shelter belt of trees that my grandfather planted.

And then my sister and I emigrated back, from the city to the country, to the roots of our ancestral home in this United States.

I'm in awe at those who had the courage to launch from the land of their birth—it was the risk of a lifetime. I admire those immigrants here who have been able to keep their land in the family name. And I'm so impressed with those who have stayed on the land through the difficult years—it's another big gamble.

The waves of immigrants that come over our country's shores today have different origin. They come from Mexico, from Vietnam, from India. Their faces are not nearly so apparent in the country as they are in California. Every group brings something of their origin, which in the end, melts into the common pool and we are all changed.

When you emigrate from one country to another there's really no turning back. Even my move from California to Kansas feels that way. The last time I was back in California I knew in my heart that I couldn't return to what I'd left behind.

Even if I *could* return, I've changed, and my point of origin has changed. Time moves us on, and decision-by-decision we create a new life.

And here I am, back at the beginning, feeling some times like an immigrant in a strange land, as I build a life on the prairie and spend another day in the country.

Clinton Hanschu stands in front of the Market he and his wife Frances owned until 2000. After Strickler's store burned to the ground in 1955 this was the only grocery store in town and owned by a succession of town folk. The building now houses The Ramona Cafe. Circa 1996

Pepper, Please

Having grown up in the country my dad hoarded toilet paper. When we moved our parents from Oregon to Kansas in 2002, we packed a complete moving carton full of toilet paper that they had stored in the garage, "just in case."

It's because our parents grew up in the days of the Great Depression where money was scarce and toilet paper almost non-existent.

You know what they used for toilet paper? Catalogs. Have you ever tried to use that slick, stiff paper? Even I remember it well, as part of the experience of visiting Grandma's outhouse. If the Sears and Roebuck catalog ran out, they resorted to corn cobs, I hear—although I never experienced that indignity.

I must admit that I have a stash of toilet paper myself. It's not because I fear running out, and having to use catalogs or junk mail, it's just that I have found a brand that I like and every store doesn't carry it.

This brand of toilet paper is nurturing, it's soft, and it has aloe in it. It's about as far from catalogs or corn cobs as you can get.

When I first brought home my cushy paper we had a small problem. "It's so soft you aren't sure if it's done what toilet paper is supposed to do," my sister moaned, "and in the middle of the night, I don't like guessing!"

Toilet paper is one of those topics that often generates humorous stories. I've got an old-time story to tell you, and it's true.

My Aunt Frieda worked at Strickler's Store in Ramona when she was a teenager. One day old Mr. Sader came in and said to her, "I vant sum pepper."

"Pepper?" said Frieda trying to understand the German brogue and the request.

He nodded and she retrieved a can of black pepper from the shelf behind her.

"Here you are," she said.

"No pepper! PEPPER," he emphasized the word and said it louder, thinking that would clarify.

Aunt Frieda reached for other cans of spice; she added red pepper to the black pepper already on the counter.

" I vant vite pepper," he said with irritation as Frieda scanned the shelves in bewilderment.

" Ach, gimme sum toilet pepper!" he finally blurted.

The last time I went to the market to get my soft, cushy aloe toilet paper, they'd changed the recipe and added something else to make it even more appealing: vitamin E *and* chamomile. Really?

I felt like Mr. Sader in Strickler's Mercantile. I wanted to holler, "Ach, yust gimme sum toilet pepper!" Pray tell, why do I need toilet tissue with an antioxidant, and a calming sleepy-time herbal tea in it?

It's another day in the country and my grandpa wouldn't believe this toilet paper dilemma. "Who needs all that fancy stuff?" Grandpa would have said, shaking his head. After all, he already knew the secret for crushing up those catalog pages, and working them over in his hand until they were as soft as a baby's butt before he applied them to his own.

A tribute to our grandfathers: A.G. Schubert's shoes and Solomon Ehrhardt's picture. Solomon always repaired the family shoes.

You Might Need That!

My Aunt Gertie is a saver; she saves everything. I caught her the other evening saving clippings from all the local newspapers.

"I've gotten myself a new scrapbook," she says in a semi-embarrassed tone of voice, "Hopefully, I'm going to put these—she motions to the basket full of clippings—into here," and she pats the new black book. Then she grins. This lady has made an art out of saving things.

You'd like to be her grandchild because she has a special notebook for each of them where she keeps their pictures, their artwork, their achievements and even their letters. She has notebooks full of historical things and boxes crammed with family history. In order to cover her wide interests she even has a notebook called "This and That." We end up in "This and That" quite often.

Uncle Hank demanded a moratorium on saving things when the last building on their property was crammed to the hilt. When we came to town, she began going through her storehouses and giving us things she'd saved for us to use in our home.

"There's an old cupboard out in the shed that used to be your great-grandma's." That cupboard was moldering away in the garage with tools and oil cans stored in it, and because she knew its history, Aunt Gertie decided to restore it, and began to strip the paint.

Aunt Gertie wore out before the cupboard was finished and we were thrilled to take up the care and keeping of this treasured family heirloom. We painted parts of it, saved some of the original color on the doors for historical purposes, and installed it in our living room.

Our family saves stories the same way Aunt Gertie saves trivia. We had heard the story about this cupboard before, but love to hear our relatives retell it, again and again. "Every year on our birthday Grandma would bake us a cake," Aunt Anna, the family matriarch, explains, "and your great-grandmother had quite a few grandchildren," she adds this so we will appreciate the enormity of the task.

"And those darn birthday cakes always tasted like Palmolive soap," Uncle Hank says taking up the story. "It's because grandma always kept her soap in that there cupboard," he motions to our new treasure, "and then she'd bake the birthday cake and store it in there, too." The warm, fresh cake soaking up the pungent smell of soap—he shakes his head and crinkles his nose remembering the odd mix of flavors.

Now, when guests come to our house, we keep the story—and Great-Grandma—alive by retelling the story of the birthday cakes that tasted like soap.

"You see how important it is to save things?" Aunt Gertie says with an impish grin. "You just never know when you might need it."

My grandma Schubert was evidently not a saver. She was a practical, pragmatic woman dedicated to doing things, not just saving things. When she moved out of the family home on the farm, and prepared for retirement in the city (Ramona), she had a great big bonfire out in the yard.

"She was heaping things on it to burn," Aunt Gertie remembers, "and I was a newlywed and a little shy about saying anything, but every time she'd turn her back I would snatch something from the fire."

In the process Aunt Gertie saved a lot of things including our great grandmother's diary. Yes, it's written in High German and none of us can read it, but we can recognize a name every now and then, and enjoy touching the pages and imagining what she might have said.

On a shelf in my house sets a pair of my grandfather's black high top shoes. Yes, Aunt Gertie saved them, too, and we rediscovered them one day when we were going through her treasures. "Take them," she said and we did.

At least once a year I pull those boots down from the shelf and polish them until I can see my face reflected in the shine. As I rub my hands over those old shoes, the memories tumble through my mind. Meanwhile, it's another day in the country and that's another story for another day.

Erich Utech proudly poses with his 1950 Ford truck, still running and still in use. Circa 2001

What's With Feed Caps?

So when was the last time you saw a country man outside, in Marion County, without a hat on? What's the deal? Are they born with them?

"Almost," a neighbor lady laughed, "I've got a picture of my little boy still in diapers wearing his dad's big hat."

Hat wearing is such a common occurrence in the country that the term "a farmer's tan," (which I do know means that the top half of your face is white because it's shaded by the hat, while the bottom half is brown) was coined. I also realize that sometimes you don't recognize a man in church on Sunday when he's got his hat off, and his hair is all combed.

"Who is that?" asked Paula, our part-time postmaster, "pointing to a picture on our office wall. "I've never seen *him* without his hat on!"

"How does this hat phenomena happen," I asked Paula. After all, she's lived in the country all of her life.

"I guess it's because men wear feed caps and little boys start wearing them, too," she says. "They start out young."

"And you'd better *not* walk into the John Deere place with an International hat on either," adds another informant, "unless you want to spur on the competition and see if they'll give you one of their hats, too."

Hats are a country trademark. Through the years, it seems to me that the only thing that's changed with this hat-wearing business is the style of hats worn.

In my father's era straw hats were used for protection from the glaring heat. Then it became almost a blue-collar stigma. Dad was quick to trade in the straw hat for a dress hat befitting a preacher.

My grandpa Schubert, a short, dapper man with a handlebar mustache, loved wearing a huge black Stetson cowboy hat. It became his trademark—the hat almost wider than the man.

These days, it's feed caps. In the city they call them baseball caps, but in the country they bear the mark of their maker: STIHL, John Deere, International.

"What else?" I call out to my buddy Tooltime Tim.

"There's *all kinds*," he says with a touch of impatience at my ignorance,

"You get company hats, equipment hats, seed hats, feed hats—*free* hats," he adds with a grin. That seems to be the best part.

"And the best thing about feed caps is that they don't blow off in the wind," says my friend Benny, always the practical man.

When Tooltime Tim and I took a recent trip to California it seemed like a journey into another time zone.

"When we land in California you've got to leave that cap off," I instructed Tim. "Unless guys are going to a ball game they just don't wear caps in California—we want you to blend in!"

We laughed at the notion of Tim "blending in," but he cooperated even if it about killed him. He did pack the cap in his suitcase, just in case. After all, that hat was protection, it was better than sunglasses to cut the glare, and it was a shield from sunburn. And we were asking the supreme sacrifice—take it off?

"He should have left it on," said my friend Mary Alice when she heard this story. "In fact, *everybody* should be wearing a hat these days for protection from the sun."

Well, it's another day in the country, and while I don't see all that many women with hats on, perhaps we'd better start a trend. I'd better get me one of those feed caps.

Lauren Brunner rests his hands on the bib of his overalls in a familiar pose. Circa 1992

Over All It's Overalls!

Did you know that people have been working and playing in overalls since the 1700s? They were one of the first mass-produced pieces of clothing and worn by slaves, railroad workers, farmers, college students, hippies, kids, oldsters, musicians, and artists.

Even the color of overalls has been significant through the years with painters wearing white, farmers blue or brown and railway workers sporting pin stripes.

When we first started coming out to Kansas, I never knew any of this overall history. All I knew was that when we flew into the Wichita Airport from San Francisco, the luggage area was sprinkled with men dressed in overalls picking up their kids or grandkids from the plane.

My sister and I would chuckle and say, "Yep, we're back in Kansas." We were country novices then, and amused at the change of scenery. For sure, you would never see so many overalls and feed caps in California.

Our neighbor Erich always wore overalls, except on Sunday. Every Monday his weekly wash hung on the line: two pair of overalls, two shirts, and two pair of socks blowing in the breeze.

I've been told that there was an old farmer in Lincolnville who used to come into Tiemeier's Store every spring, peel off his old overalls and underwear, buy a new pair of each, put them on and walk out the door, leaving the discards behind. In the fall, he'd come back in, buy new long winter underwear, a second pair of overalls to put on over the ones he already owned and he was set for the rest of the year. Now that's a simplified wardrobe that makes Erich's two-overalls-a-week regime seem extravagant.

When my father left the country, he also left his overalls behind. I don't believe I ever saw him wear another pair after we moved away from the little Scully farm west of Ramona. He was going off to college to study to be a minister and the wardrobe was about to make a drastic shift.

Dad wore suits and white shirts almost every day of his life from then on. When he wanted to be casual he wore slacks—rarely jeans, and never overalls.

When we came back to Ramona and bought The Ramona House many years ago, Uncle Hank took one look at the old California clothes we had brought with us for painting and promptly offered us a pair of overalls.

"You girls will have more paint on you than on them there boards," he said with a grin. "These might help."

But alas, it took a wizard to undo those hooky-things and I was constantly tangled in straps when I headed for the bathroom. Furthermore, the long legs were hot, so we just draped the Henry Schubert Memorial Overalls in the corner of the dining room for display.

While we never warmed to overalls, Ramona's newest resident thinks they're the cat's meow! Jim Thompson, moved from California to Kansas, and with only three or four months of country life under his belt, he showed up the other day wearing brand new overalls.

"Whoa," I exclaimed, "you've got overalls!" While he still may not feel like a seasoned country resident, he certainly looks the part.

"These are the most comfortable things I've ever worn," he enthused, showing off his new togs. "I just love them. There's a pocket for everything and places to hang tools. These are the greatest invention ever!"

It's another day in the country and overalls have a new fan, "I may never wear anything but overalls from now on," Jim says.

A stay at our Bed and Breakfast, Cousin's Corner, (on the corner of Fourth and D Streets) is like returning to grandma's house. Circa 2003

The Ceiling Register

In 1995 the old Lutheran parsonage in Ramona became ours—although it had been many years since it served as the pastor's residence. It was a stately old two-story home with a clattery stairs and bedrooms on the second floor. I must admit that one reason I liked the house was those noisy stairs.

Hearing kids run up and down the stairs just transported me back to my childhood. The sound even stirred my mother's memories since she used to run up and down those very stairs when she was a child, because her good friend, the preacher's daughter, lived there.

To my delight, in the process of cleaning up the house we named Cousin's Corner, I lifted a tattered old rug and discovered a ceiling register upstairs. It no longer functioned, having succumbed to a lowered ceiling in the room below, but I vowed to liberate that register some day.

Just seeing the ceiling vent took me back to being six years old, laying on my tummy looking down through the fancy grate in Grandma's house, while the older cousins played in the upstairs rooms.

While I adored playing with my cousins, I loved even more watching my parents, grandparents, aunts and uncles below me—when they didn't know six-year-old ears were listening. I could listen by the hour.

Listening through the ceiling register was like being an angel sitting on a cloud, watching people live their lives, oblivious to any higher presence. There was something so satisfying about the hum of conversation below.

I relished the sound of family voices conversing back and forth—of Uncle John telling a story that made people laugh, Uncle Walter nodding in his easy chair while the buzz of family went on around him, Aunt Erna putting away dishes in the china cupboard while she hummed a tune, and my mother cleaning the table and setting things in order.

No one seemed to notice, but I registered every scene through the magic little hole in the ceiling. I watched as the adult women gathered around Grandma's china cupboard, looking at a photograph displayed there, and discussing a new addition to the family. Their sister had died. Their brother-in-law had remarried. This new woman in our lives had a child.

The sisters gazed at the picture as the family code danced in the air between them: "Hear no evil, see no evil, speak no evil."

The leader of the pack finally announced. "Mama's invited them to Sunday dinner. You'll all meet her then."

I learned as I listened, how the Schubert family fluffed their feathers, spread their wings, settled in to claim their own. I gleaned with only a nod from my grandmother what was acceptable to discuss and what wasn't.

Occasionally, I couldn't resist letting the adults below know that I was up at that hole in the ceiling peering down on them. I'd whisper, "Grandpa, look here?"

If Grandma saw our conspiracy she'd say, "Careful what you talk about, girls. Little pitchers have big ears," and the aunts would look up to see if it was *their* naughty child eaves dropping on the adults.

Well, it's another day in the country and I'm back in Kansas, more sixty than six. We finally tore out that false ceiling that the previous owners had installed under the guise of home improvements. I needed that ceiling register to do its job, even if the heat bill is higher.

The next generation needs the chance to listen through that ceiling grate in Cousin's Corner—to know their family, watch them interact, and react, just as I learned about mine—with their faces pressed down and their ears tuned to the hum of life going on below.

Dirt roads are like driving in soft bath powder until it starts to rain—then stay off! Circa 2002

Taking a Chance

I'm an avid chance-taker—like some people are sports enthusiasts. In fact, taking a chance *is* a sporting event for me. These chances aren't dangerous, hurtful, completely foolish, or potentially devastating. They are minor little mini-chances.

For instance, I love taking back roads instead of paved highways. That's just a little chance-y, they tell me, because you can pick up nails, breathe too much dust, or meet another vehicle unexpectedly. But there's just something so adventurous about taking the road less traveled.

The other day I needed to go to town and decided to take a chance on a shortcut even though it was threatening to rain. After all, Paint Road has only two miles of dirt road in a six-mile stretch, and it wasn't even sprinkling, yet. That was a chance worth taking.

When my sister raised her eyebrows at my choice of roads I rhapsodized, "That dirt stretch is so wonderful to drive on—sweet and soft like velvet, as relaxing as a swing in the hammock under a shade tree, as quiet as a whisper, as refreshing to the ears (after the gravel stretch) as cold lemonade is to your tongue on a hot day."

I could have gone on, but that would have been taking more of a chance than I thought wise since Jess prefers pavement.

Of course, I pride myself in knowing enough to stay off those dirt roads when it's been raining. However, being a one-time city slicker, I didn't know the part about staying away if there's even a *chance* of rain.

As we drove north along Paint Road, I watched the gathering storm clouds, heard thunder, and saw a few bolts of lightening.

"Hmm," I thought to myself, not wanting to disturb the other occupants in the car, "I wonder if it is really going to rain?" No sooner thought than heard—raindrops on my roof. Evidently the rain was coming our direction—hadn't thought of that possibility.

I still wasn't terribly perturbed when the gravel on Paint Road came to an end, and we *slid* on to the stretch of the road that was dirt only. After all, I've lived in the Colorado mountains and navigated some pretty treacherous winter roads, but I quickly discovered that the slickest mountain pass was nothing in comparison to one slightly damp Kansas dirt road.

My Honda swerved in the mud, fishtailed, threatened to completely change direction, staggered like a drunken sailor, slid sideways, and then prayers started ascending from the nine-year-old in the back seat.

"We're going to end up in the ditch," Emily wailed between "Hail Marys."

My sister said, "Think positive!" as she perched on the front seat in her high heels. She knew rescue would be a long time coming if *she* had to walk down the mud road for help.

From the back seat Emily took my sister's advice and began chanting, "We're going to make it, we're going to make it!" I wasn't so sure we were.

Of course, I'd like to think that my expert driving ability was what got us safely back on the highway, but Tooltime Tim tells me, "It was that Honda's front wheel drive." Ah, shucks.

And with a grin on his face, Tim admonishes, "Don't go near dirt roads even if all you hear is thunder; nothing is slicker than dust with a few rain drops on it!"

"I hope you've learned your lesson," my sister intoned loosening her white knuckles from the door handle once we'd reached safety.

When we got to Herington we headed straight for the car wash. We were covered with so much mud that we could only see out the little section of windshield smeared by the wipers, and I didn't want to take the chance of meeting anyone I knew.

It's another day in the country, and we've been worried ever since that slippery ride, that whoever drove down Paint Road when it was finally safe to traverse, took one look at the swerving tracks and muttered, "This had to be those girls from California."

The tulips behind Cousin's Corner bring joy to our soul every spring! Circa 2003

Four O'Clocks and Tulips

The seed catalogs have begun to arrive in the mail tempting me to dream of spring while Ramona is still ice-bound. As I once again experience the rigors of a Kansas winter I agree with the Frenchman Albert Camus, that, "In the midst of winter, I've finally learned there is in me an invincible summer."

It must run in the family because my uncle Hank has been performing the yearly ritual of bringing his amaryllis bulbs upstairs from the basement to set beside the floor furnace. He, too, is dreaming of spring as he invites the bulbs to send up green shoots, waiting for that one, long, wonderful shoot to appear promising lovely blooms by Easter. He has become, at 85, the amaryllis expert in town.

My grandma Schubert had flowers that she carried through the winter, too, babying her Christmas cactus that bloomed only once a year, and wisteria that she wintered in the cellar and carried up to the porch in spring so that their fragrance filled the summer air. My grandmother loved to garden. She grew flowers during drought or pestilence, heat waves or gully washes. Young, old, pregnant or arthritic, Grandmother kept right on growing flowers.

When she could no longer grow flowers outdoors because of cold winter weather, she drew tulip shapes on bright colored scraps of cloth and decorated her house. There were tulips marching across the bottom of the kitchen curtains. Tulips bloomed on plump velvet pillows that rested on the divan. Tulip appliqués adorned the kitchen dish towels. She stitched tulip shapes on velvet scraps and covered bricks for door stops. One of her creations still props open my bedroom door, though the tulips are so worn they've almost disappeared.

Aunt Anna remembers Grandma telling stories about winter in Poland when *her* mother would cut out bright colored flowers from paper and stick them onto the window glass, so that when they looked out onto the bleak gray winter landscape there was something bright shining in their windows. A transplant to American soil, Grandmother kept the tradition going.

So many flowers hold memories of Grandma's wealthy garden legacy. A brilliant orange trumpet vine grew by her kitchen door. Huge blue morning glories spilled over the window ledge, smiling at the early morning sun as Grandma worked in the garden. The lilac bushes beside the porch sent their fragrance into the warm spring air out on the farm, and plate-sized dahlias were the showpiece of her garden, even though they had to be staked, babied, protected and cared for in the mid-western heat.

By the time I came along in the family line-up, photographs show a tired Grandma. She had struggled against the odds, birthed nine children, cared for extra family and friends, lived through dust storms and tornadoes, survived the Great Depression, and *still* never said a discouraging word.

I wonder if she grew flowers for soul food, as I do? Were the four o'clocks, with their fleeting evening fragrance, a reminder of her abundance? Were the tulip shapes proof that life was more than just fulfilling duties? Were the pampered dahlias a symbol that she was indeed a wealthy woman?

When winter winds blew snow over the flower beds obliterating any signs of four o'clocks in her yard, when the trumpet vine's thick brown cord-like stems were all that was clinging to her door post, and the morning glories were frozen on the windmill's frame, Grandma could always pick up her scraps of cloth and create tulip shapes.

The tulips dancing on the curtain borders soothed her soul on a long-ago day in the country, and reminded her that even in the dead of winter, spring can always be found in your heart.

We planted these old-fashioned phlox in our yard at The Ramona House in honor of Grandma Schubert. Circa 1994

Grandma's Rototiller

At this time of the year, the Schubert/Bentz families start digging around in the dirt. It's part of our heritage. It's genetic. It's built into our DNA.

Everyone didn't get it, just like everyone doesn't have brown eyes; but a goodly portion of us are infected with the gardening bug.

When some of the cousins were together last month, we were already itching to be planting and began to talk about rototillers. "I've got a new one," said my cousin Gary. "It's a sweet little thing."

"I *need* a new one," I confessed. "Dad's old rototiller is too heavy for me to handle and Tooltime Tim doesn't even want to start it up for fear it will be one more thing he ends up doing. I've got to get one of those girl-tillers that are light weight and easy to start."

We sat reminiscing about gardens, tools and what we wanted to plant this year, and our thoughts turned to our grandmother who always had a big garden. "Wouldn't Grandma have loved having one of these new little tillers," I said.

"What do you mean?" interjected my cousin Keith. "*I was Grandma's tiller!*" We all laughed at Keith's exclamation as he went on, "Every spring when Grandma was ready to plant, Dad would send me up to spade her garden for her."

Keith was probably nine years old when he first became Grandma's rototiller and it continued into his teens until she died. Being Grandma Schubert's rototiller was one more thing we missed out on because we didn't live in the country.

Our genetics for growing things began over a hundred years ago in Kansas when my grandfather moved here from Illinois with all of his worldly possessions in a railroad car including fence posts, horses and a plow—the 1800s version of a rototiller, I guess. No, take that back—the horses were the forerunners of the tractor. The kids were the rototillers, eh?

Albert Schubert married Auguste Bentz and proceeded to bring nine children into the world—most all of them gardeners who have to get their hands in the dirt come spring.

The other day, my mother Martha (who is 88) came home from the grocery store and said, "I bought some onion sets—I just couldn't help myself—even though I don't have any place to plant them."

"Plant them in a pot," I suggested. But, she already had her pots full of flowers, shielding them from frost and cold spring winds. Those pots were blooming with the hopefulness that spring engenders.

"You just put them in *your* garden," she said.

Every spring, I watch the gardeners in Kansas to give me cues as to when it's safe to plant. Coming from California, where we could plant something almost anytime, I am in need of continuing education. Kink planted peas and radishes ages ago. Betty has potatoes in, of course, and I think she has tomatoes hiding under buckets.

Yesterday, I met a world-class gardener in Marion, whose garden I always envy. He had built himself a contraption out of 1x4s to pull through his garden so that his rows are as straight as an arrow. I stopped the car and watched his progress.

"So what do you have planted?" I called out.

"Potatoes, onions, corn," he gestured to several rows. "I always start some corn early, just in case it doesn't freeze!" And he grinned like a seasoned dirt-gambler, who takes a chance on nature every year.

"Maybe I need me one of those row-makers," I told Tooltime Tim, later.

"You wouldn't use it," he said. "You're too impatient—you won't even put up a string!"

He's right! But I did get me a cute little rototiller that is just the right size to fit between the rows, even if they're crooked. Tim put it together, filled it with gas and fired it up.

"Now you try it," he commanded. I was ecstatic! I could *start* that tiller all by myself. "You don't have to run it full bore," Tim hollered as I took off. No office work for me! Taxes can wait! It's another day in the country and this country girl is going to play in the dirt!

This old home is symbolic of so many that stand empty on the prairie. Circa 2000

Country Life is Unforgiving

"Country life can be harsh and unforgiving," said my sister, shaking her head sadly at the word that our newest residents were leaving Ramona. "You make a mistake and people will never forget it!"

She's right! You can dream all you want of country living with idyllic notions of warmth, nostalgia, charm, camaraderie and simplicity (ala Mayberry R.F.D.) but reality with its twists and turns, misunderstandings and mistakes, suddenly looms.

In the country, make a foolish mistake and you can lose your life. Make a poor judgment call and you can lose your shirt, a series of bad choices and you've lost your reputation—which is probably your most important asset. And, to boot, everyone knows!

In the country, there is no such thing as anonymity unless you are most assuredly a hermit. The irony is that if you choose to be isolated the populace will probably make up what they don't know. People just talk!

That penchant for talk in the country and the content of conversations is what fired our passion for writing in *The Marion County Record*. "Since country folk will talk, let's give them good things to report to one another," we said.

"Let's write about good deeds, good things, good news in Ramona and then the general tone of country chatter will be more positive." It isn't that negative things don't happen in our own little Mayberry. We just don't put it in print.

Country news doesn't really need a newspaper, however, to get around. If the Sheriff drives over the railroad tracks, within minutes most everyone in town knows where he stopped and guesses why.

Let your kids run without supervision, or discipline them strictly and the whole town will have an opinion about your parenting skills, or lack thereof.

Do a good deed, be charitable and kind, ask forgiveness for your mistakes and we'll probably not hear a word of it. However, make a mistake, shoot off your mouth, or cross paths with the wrong person and you will be the source of endless surmising and maybe even lawsuits.

We've sometimes wondered if a manual should be published on Country Living and a copy given to any newcomer into town. There would be all the numbers and names of whom to contact for utilities and hook-ups—things have definitely gotten more complicated since the days we first moved here when all you had to do was watch for Bob in the KPL truck and tell him you'd moved to town.

Perhaps there should be lists of folks to get to know and whom to avoid, tips on good neighbor policies, and lists of things country folk already know and just take for granted, like:

#1 Don't drive on dirt roads after it rains.
#2 Fix your roof before you fix up the inside of the house.

"That's just common sense. Everybody knows that," says Tooltime Tim, our most practical country cohort.

"No, they don't," I counter. "City life is very different from country living."

When we first came to the country we had our aunts and uncles as our handbook. We coasted on their reputation and had a safe haven under their wings. We still benefit from this kinship.

It's another day in the country and a recent move-in added a bit of advice for our mythical *Handbook for Potential Newcomers*.

"If you want to make a go of it here," he said, "and feel like you belong, you'd better have someone buried in the cemetery."

These fine horses are owned and trained by Mr. Buhler who has a farm just off Highway 4. Circa 2002

Whoa! Team

Yesterday on the way to Salina I saw farmer Buhler out in his field with a matched team of Percheron draft horses pulling a manure spreader behind them. Maybe it was the way the sun backlit the team and the driver's straw hat. Perhaps it was the way the wind picked up the contents of the spreader and fanned it out behind them. Really, it was pure unadulterated nostalgia that hit me. It was a scene from over fifty years ago, being played out before my eyes.

I was a kid again, and that was my grandpa out there with the team—working horses long after everyone else used tractors.

Grandpa had a tractor, but he didn't trust it. Something was always breaking down, the fool thing would run out of gas, and it was noisy—all reasons enough to settle for working with the team. He knew the needs and the habits of his horses. They would work as long as he could, plodding across the field in a straight line.

For row crops, especially, these horses were ideal. They walked at a steady pace, "You can work the crops better," he'd say. "These guys with their tractors and expensive equipment want to run around out there all over the field and be done with it. Not me!"

Farmer Buhler talked with his horses like my grandpa did. "C'mon there Bruce, let's go!" And Bruce stepped up in the traces. Let's see a tractor be *that* responsive.

Grandpa could cluck to his horses when he was pitching hay on the wagon and they'd walk along without even a hand on the lines. "Back, Jim, back." And Jim would lead his buddy in backing up the hay wagon.

"Whoa," he'd say and they would stop.

Sometimes, Grandpa would let me drive. I'm not real sure who was leading whom, but with my hands on the lines I always thought I was in control. It was the high point of my day of trekking around after Grandpa on a hot summer day, to be able to drive those horses home. They knew the way quite well without me, but I didn't think so.

I loved everything about those horses. I loved their smell and the smell of the harness. I loved the feel of their hot breath on my hand when I fed them oats. I loved the sturdy strength of them as I leaned against Jim's side as they drank at the stock tank.

These were the only horses Grandpa had, and as long as I can remember I dreamed of not just driving horses but riding them.

You can imagine what a stretch it was for my cousin and me to ride old Jim. He was almost as broad as he was wide. There was no such thing as a saddle or a saddle blanket.

My mother insisted I always wear a dress. So in dresses I rode, legs parallel to the ground, swatting off horse flies and enduring the chafing of horse hide on bare skin as long as I could. We were always sore afterward, and so I'd settle for just driving the team for a few days.

Jim's fastest gait was a trot—and a very bumpy and reluctant trot at that. We'd trot (on the way home) but mostly he was geared up in true draft horse style with a walk that was slow, slower and slowest. I used to get so impatient at his lack of speed.

As I watched farmer Buhler move off across his field the other day with yet another load of manure, my camera clicking to record the scene, I smiled at the slow rocking pace of this lovely team of Percherons. Mr. Buhler told me that these horses originated in the LaPerche District of France and legend tells us that Joan of Arc rode a Percheron into battle.

There was something soothing about the horses' pace. There was something peaceful in the motion, the whir of the spreader tines spreading fertilizer, the creak of leather, the clink of a chain, the meadowlarks singing from the fence row, the farmer softly talking to his team. I couldn't keep from grinning.

I wanted to stay rooted to that spot for a while, as the memories of my past mingled with sweet scenes from another day in the country.

"Are we really safer here?" we ask each other. Here's Pat, Cousin Keith, Aunt Gertie and Uncle Hank in their partial basement—it's only about eight square feet shared with reinforcement timbers and a sump pump. But, hey, we had a radio! Circa 1995

Tornado Watch

Gertie's grandson came skidding up to our gate in the car, "Grandma says a tornado is coming and you better get over to the house so we can go downstairs in their basement."

"Really?" I said, "that serious?" And even as I questioned, the town siren went off, signaling the inhabitants of Ramona that there was indeed a tornado too close for comfort and they should take cover.

Jess was out the door. "Come on, Pat," she said, "don't mess around with this."

I'd been watching the sky turn gray-green, but I hadn't checked the horizon. "I want to see what the sky looks like on the edge of town," I said.

As we drove to the outskirts of Ramona where we could see the skyline, we could indeed see that the horizon was dark and ominous but it looked to me like it was going to pass to the east of town—we weren't directly in its path.

"Let's get going," said my sister. "You've looked long enough."

By this time the rain was coming down in serious fashion—lashing out at us as we ran from the car into Aunt Gertie's house.

"Open the cellar door," Aunt Gertie commanded. "It says right there on the TV," she pointed at the bottom of the screen, "'RAMONA take cover,' so you all get into the cellar!"

"Is there a light down there?" Jess wanted to know.

There was. Down the rickety stairs we went, brushing cobwebs out of our way. When we looked up at our relatives' crooked old house from underneath in the cellar, Jess nudged me and said, "Are you sure we are *safer* down *here*?"

"That's the theory," I said laughing.

"This is no laughing matter," Jess countered. "I don't like it! *At all!*"

Aunt Gertie descended the stairs clutching her transistor radio so we could keep apprised of the storm. "Otherwise how would you know when to come up?" she said.

We sat huddled in a circle in the cramped, damp cellar on rickety stools, an old box, a chair, with our backs against the wall, not sure what to do next. We listened as the storm howled above us.

"Do you have your billfold?" My cousin Keith asked. I didn't.

"There's a check list of things you should take with you," Aunt Gertie said, "Billfold, flashlight, radio, water..." She was going down the list.

"Did anyone put playing cards on the list?" we wanted to know. "This could get a little tedious just sitting here. How long do we stay?"

"We stay until they give us the all clear," said Aunt Gertie decisively. She was almost enjoying this family togetherness.

"Micah," I said in my sweetest voice, "do you know where the cards are upstairs?"

Micah was my cousin's teenage son, and he was willing to take a risk for playing cards. He creaked open the cellar door, pushing it above his head, and tentatively looking around—obviously the house was still there.

"Here I go," he hollered to all of us waiting below, "don't leave without me," he joked as he scurried to find the cards.

We felt just a little guilty sending a teenager into a danger zone just to find playing cards, so we added a couple other things to the list. "Micah, any chance you could bring down some water—better yet Pepsi?"

By now he was getting reckless—he'd made three trips up the cellar stairs. When he finally reappeared, feet first descending into the cellar he was stepping very carefully. In true butler-fashion he'd put on an apron, had a towel over his arm, and on a tray he not only had Pepsi, but glasses filled with ice. In a most dignified manner he said, "Is there anything else I could get for you folks tonight?" We dissolved into laughter.

We stayed in the cellar until the radio said the storm had passed to the east of us. We breathed a collective sigh of relief and came back up into the humid house, opened the front door, and inhaled the now cool, rain-washed country air.

"Whew, that there was too close for comfort," said Uncle Hank, as he sank into his easy chair. So *this* was what it was like to spend another day in the country!

Aunt Naomi tells me that her mother had an old gas iron like this one and always had it "fired up and ready" for her to use after school. Circa 1994

The Country Code

There's a different scale of measurement in the country than in the city. In the city, commerce sets the tone and demands a forty-hour week or a workday that extends until the work is done. There is predictability from nine to five, end of the month, vacations, and a fiscal year.

In the country, nature dominates the timetable with sunrise and darkness, summer and fall, heat and freezing weather. One can never quite predict when things change in the country.

The wary and the watchful are most often right. And rightness is very important in the country with many a "I coulda told ya," or "I had a notion to say" which denotes higher power, which, I guess, tends to put you one step closer to a Deity who is all-knowing.

What is saved and what is thrown away is measured on a different scale in the country. Old pieces of furniture that have gathered dust in the same corner for a century are set outside to molder and rot and referred to as "oh, that old thing," while folks in the city covet those rustic dressers and chairs, label them antiques, and pay a pretty penny for them.

I was just a kid when I saw Grandma put her old pump organ outside on the south side of the house. In the house, we'd been cautioned to "be careful now," but outside, we pushed the keys and pedaled in non-harmonic bliss, even with mud on our feet.

While the pump organ fell from grace, an extension cord with the business-end missing was saved "just in case" you needed it to fix something, no matter how ragged the transmission of electricity. When you have to drive fifteen miles to find a hardware store, saving string, screws, pieces of tin, hunks of old metal, and baling wire comes in handy.

There's a measurement in the social code that city dwellers have trouble tracking. How is someone deemed acceptable or found questionable in a town filled with quaint old characters and eccentrics?

As former city dwellers, we try to be cautious. We don't want folks to look completely askance at these girls from California. It's obvious we are "move-ins" as Aunt Gertie says.

"You girls just don't know!" is a phrase we hear quite often when we ask for explanation of the cadence and code of small town life. "You just don't know!" And we don't—but we're learning!

Some things we accept—as in everyone knowing your business—and some things we refuse to accept—as in people "spooling up" and turning fiction into fact.

We do know that in a small town you need to keep your property up—as in cleaning away trash and painting—and your weeds down. The older generation who have lived their lifetime around here tend their small acreage with care, and a mowed lawn is part of your integrity as a good neighbor. Any added embellishments like flowers and picket fences are appreciated but not necessary, and may be seen as "putting on the dog," so to speak.

While I write, I hear lawn mowers starting up and I've learned the drill. It's another day in the country and it's time to mow. You just can't have your neighbors' grass too much shorter that your own, it upsets the community equilibrium.

From the back yard of Cousin's Corner we can see the park through the trees as spring arrives. Circa 2002

Spring's Busting Out All Over

In California spring arrives gently. The temperature doesn't change all that drastically from winter to spring—it just warms up a little. And then one day you notice that the wild plum trees have begun to bloom along the roadside. There is a flurry of activity in the vineyards as last minute pruning is done, and mustard begins to bloom, turning the bed of the Napa Valley to bright yellow as far as your eye can see. It's really quite beautiful.

By contrast, spring in Kansas hits like gangbusters! One day it's winter, and ka-boom the next day it's spring. There's a raw beauty here in the country that I love as the fields turn from brown to green one day, and the wheat seems to be standing a foot high the next.

The weathermen switch into an even higher gear with Doppler reports and tornado warnings. Winter and summer seasons battle it out on our horizon as clouds tumble and expand. Low or high pressure gets into the act doing whatever pressure systems do best, and we stand on the hill west of town and watch the show. Nature is out of control.

Everything is in heat! The neighbors' dogs are procreating. I begin a mental tally of Ramona's expanding dog population, and shake my head in dismay. It seems like nature just has its way in the country.

In the Napa Valley, while it looks like a semi-rural area, nature is very much subdued by asphalt pavement, chemicals, and neutering clinics. Here in Kansas, the rule of thumb seems to be rampant reproduction and survival of the fittest.

There are three strange tomcats in the yard vying for the attention of one young female. I root for the longhaired black cat because we already have too many generic tiger-striped cats in town. Watching the cats posture, pose and move in slow motion makes me think I'm watching a small-scale version of mating rituals on *Wild Kingdom.*

Last year's male kittens stand on the fringes taking lessons and yowling their concern. I feel like joining in on the lament, because there are already several female cats within eyesight that are about to give birth.

Even the trees are getting into the act. "Every one of those *helicopters* that lands on my porch means another one of those messy trees will try and come up in my flower bed," laments my aunt. Her porch is littered with seed pods and she isn't happy about it.

In my own garden, I've been trying to decipher the good from the bad. As I recall, scripture admonishes to let the good and bad seed grow together until harvest; but I don't like that idea. I want my garden to look neat and tidy. When seedlings appear in my freshly tilled soil, I hold everything suspect that isn't in a straight row, and start to hoe!

Meanwhile I'm watching in the flower beds for the poppy seed to come up that I "scattered on the snow" as instructed. The straight-row-theory of selection won't work in this case.

Our first harbinger of spring came when we were driving past Marion Lake and saw a male eagle carrying a huge tree limb toward a prospective nesting site. It was almost more than he could carry, but it attracted the attention of a young female. She was impressed, and once the limb was implanted they wheeled and cavorted high in the sky in the timeless mating dance of the species. It was mesmerizing to behold.

Early in the morning there's a cacophony of bird calls as the males sing out their boundaries and proclaim their nesting territory. The blue jays, which have set up housekeeping in a tree on the edge of our yard, do their version of bird birth control. They have an omelet every morning from some poor neighbor's nest. I see the empty fragments of robin-blue eggs or white mourning dove eggs on the road to prove the culprit guilty.

Spring is the time for rapid growth in the country as farmers attempt to work with the elements of nature, and get the seed planted in the ground between rains. There are newborn calves dropping in the fields outside of town—fresh scrubbed, tiny white faces peaking out of green prairie grass.

It's just another day in the country and Mother Nature's primordial clock is ticking—now is the time to be fruitful and multiply.

Jake Brunner uses his fingers to measure the amount of rain that he collected in his rain gauge. Circa 1995

Rain Gauges

In California, where I lived the last several decades, the weather is pretty much ignored. We go to work in buildings that are climate controlled, and you barely know the time of day, let alone what's happening outside. We have two seasons—rain and sun.

During winter rains, we act like it's not raining as we dash from car to store, because the rain is usually more like mist than like a Kansas deluge. With all that concrete, we have no such thing as serious mud.

During summer—the sunny season in California—you know from one day to the next pretty much what the weather will be like. It's going to be sunny and warm. No one really talks about it. It's not that interesting unless there is an earthquake.

In Kansas, however, the weather is always changing, so it's a constant source of comment. Furthermore, we're completely out of control—which gives us a peculiar kind of camaraderie.

One summer, early in our years of returning to Ramona, my neighbor Jim called from across the street. "How much rain did you get yesterday?"'

I wondered, right out loud, how different it could be from one side of the road to the other? It shows how naive I was!

"You've just got to get yourself a rain gauge," Jim said. "How do you expect to survive in Ramona? You won't have anything to talk about if you can't discuss the weather."

I've since learned that Jim is right. I've heard one farmer say, "We got about an inch and a quarter," and another one would say, "An inch, thirty" "Nah, inch and a quarter." This dialogue can go on and on, back and forth, no one wanting to give even a tenth of an inch until someone suggests they play cards and forget about the rain.

I've even been told that at some point in recent history, Ramona had an *official* rain gauge, residing at Hannah Sader's restaurant. I've also received the confession of at least one man, who on at least one occasion, added water to that gauge—thereby tampering with official evidence. It's probably safe for him to confess at this point, because the restaurant and Hannah are no longer here.

My neighbor, Erich, told me that rain gauges couldn't be trusted, anyhow. "You could have a gauge—the same kind of gauge—setting on one fence post, and six feet over, have another one, and they'd be different," he said. In fact, he has had that happen out on his farm. "Different every time!" he insists, which explains why Jim calls me from across the street, asking if I got more rain than he did.

I can remember Jakie Brunner relished giving out the rain statistics. Old timers tell me that Jakie always got more rain than anybody else, it was a sense of pride. "We had four inches last night," he called to me one summer from his front porch. "That son of a gun ran right over the top. Yessiree."

My aunt Anna, who keeps the family organized and categorized with births, deaths, and marriages, also keeps track of rain statistics religiously. I tease her saying she probably keeps a tally so that she can add those inches up, and when we've had enough rain she can tell the Lord to send some of this moisture to Texas.

Now that I've lived in the country for a spell I realize the elemental importance of wind patterns and rainfall. The weather decrees if you will have feast or famine, whether the wheat can be planted, when it can be harvested, and how much corn you will get per bushel in an acre. I've even been told that the recent drought is affecting calf production this spring—amazing!

Everyone experiences the weather, and it seems to me that country stalwarts have a built-in gauge to test the veracity of each other's weather comments. Did you exaggerate? Did you raise the temperature? Did you forget important elements? (They'll expect the same behavior when you talk about your husband, the economy or the local preacher.)

And so the rain came down last night, nourishing the earth, settling the dust, and creating more mud. According to the rain gauges, it came down indiscriminately on the just and the unjust, just as scripture says it should, taking no account as to whether you'd been to church last week, cheated on your income tax or talked crossly to your kids.

On top of it all, the sun came up again this morning without fail, which leaves me talking about the weather again, too, as I send up praises for another day in the country.

These cattle are quite content as they peer placidly through the fence at me.

Cottage Cheese Comes From Where?

One day, about thirty years ago, I recall having a conversation with my little daughter, Jana. It was one of those "where does it come from," talks that surfaces when children are about four years old.

She was showing off her expertise as we drove along the valley road. "I know where milk comes from," Jana said, tilting up her chin and looking at me. "From cows." And then with a glint in her eye, "And chocolate milk comes from the brown cows, right?" She knew that wasn't right, but it was good for a chuckle.

"What about cottage cheese?" I asked, "Where does that come from?"

"The store?" she countered.

"Good try!" I knew then that I needed to find some fresh whole milk so I could show my little girl the wonders of making cottage cheese—but where do you find fresh milk in a metropolitan area?

Luckily, I don't have that trouble in the country. My buddy, Jim, called the other day and said, "I've got some extra cream. You want some?"

Seems Jim wanted whipping cream to fry down and thicken so he could pour it over some delicacy he was hungry for, so he called me when he had extra.

"Sure, I'll gladly take some of that rich whole milk you got from the Hanschu's Jersey cows," I told Jim, and then I beat a path to his door to get it.

Visions of *kasenoodle* floated in my mind—fresh noodle pockets filled with a mixture of breadcrumbs, onions and cottage cheese in a cream sauce. Mmmm, good!

When I started cooking, the smell of sautéed onions and thick cream bubbling in the skillet transported me back to my mother's kitchen. To this day, Mom cooks like a German farmer's wife. Until recently, she had her own chickens, which produced fresh eggs, along with her garden full of produce. But fresh cream and fresh milk, were always a luxury unparalleled.

Walking in Mom's footsteps, it never even occurred to me to use that fresh milk (left after skimming off the cream) for cooking—I'd make cottage cheese. It's been awhile, but I remembered the process.

So last night, well after ten o'clock, I was standing at my stove gently stirring the clabbered milk as it heated. There were voices in my head as I accomplished this simple task.

I could hear my mother admonishing, "Don't heat the milk too hot!"

I could hear my grandmother fussing about someone she knew whose cottage cheese always tasted sour. "She didn't wash it long enough," she explained.

Patiently I watched the curds and whey begin to separate. Like my grandmother and mother before me, I pinched a curd between my fingers to see if it was ready for rinsing. Automatically I saved the whey. Mom sometimes used it in bread; Grandma would make something called whey soup. I fed my whey to the cats. They weren't impressed.

Grandma always poured the steaming mixture into a clean white cloth, and after she'd rinsed it well in cold clear water, she twisted the cloth shut, squeezed out what little liquid remained, and then she hung it on the clothesline.

When I went to bed my little cup of cheese was drained, rinsed, twisted tight, and hanging contentedly over the old-fashioned faucet on my kitchen sink.

As a child, I could hardly wait for that cheese to be finished. Grandma kept it in a pan in the pantry and I loved going in there and snitching a big cottage cheese curd. To me, it was more delicious than candy. One curd at a time, Gramm's cottage cheese supply would diminish, as her granddaughter delighted in every morsel.

There are so many childhood memories I could revive with my little ball of homemade cheese. I could make real *kasenoodle* or *schmierkase* like Grandma did, or I could add some cream and fresh onion greens as my mother often does, and have homemade cottage cheese as a salad with my meal. Which to choose?

It's another day in the country and as I stood at the kitchen sink eating fresh cottage cheese with salt on it, I was a little girl again in Grandma's pantry.

The Brunners are one of the oldest cattle farming families in Ramona. Patriarch Lauren Brunner is surrounded by his sons (with hats on) Kent, Tracy and Mark. Kent's son, Nolan (far left) is also part of the family business. Circa 2000

Country Continuity

It is such a country phenomena: several generations of history on the land, several sets of family with the same last name living down the road and across the field, several spots reserved in the local cemetery alongside several relatives that have gone before.

In a state like California, populated by adventurers of a more recent ilk, those layers of generations on the land are mostly missing. That layering of history is one of the things that called us back to Kansas in the first place. The loosening of those layers is also something we grieve.

Uncle Hank, whose been the hub of the Schubert family for years and years is about to become an immigrant to Colorado. He and Aunt Gertie, our local historians, whom we depend on for all kinds of tid-bits of information, are moving to be near their children.

While we understand this latest transition in our heads, our hearts are hurting. Suddenly, we'll not be able to walk two blocks down and take them goodies, or suggest a game of ten-point pitch.

It reminds me of all those who were left behind in the old country— whatever that country of origin was named—Germany for our ancestors, and now Ramona.

In my long-ago-husband's family it was Norway, and Ted sometimes told the story that had been passed down to him of his grandmother and her sisters standing on the wharf waving until the ship was a small speck on the ocean horizon. They were sending three young men to the United States— immigrating to a better place—and they knew the odds were high that they'd never see them again.

In actuality, all three boys were lost to their mother. America was a long ways away and news, at best, was foreign and disjointed. She never saw her sons again.

An Aunt told Ted this story and tears streamed down her face as she now looked at her brother's son, standing once more on Norwegian soil.

I've tried to imagine a parting of such magnitude—sending someone off that you may never see again—but not until now are we faced with such a parting in my family!

"It's life," we say to one another. "It's best!" we remind ourselves. "It's inevitable," says Uncle Hank.

In the country, we all grieve when the generations leave, and we all rejoice when they return. Our friend, Paula, had three younger generations of her offspring at the May Tea on Mother's Day weekend. She stood proudly with her daughter, granddaughter and great-granddaughters while I took a picture. Seeing four generations of lovely Fike women together again made us all smile.

That same day, three generations of Brunners were mowing the lawn at Trinity Lutheran Church. Patriarch, Lauren, was on the riding mower, his son, Tracy, had the weed eater, and Tracy's young son, Tanner, was supposed to be doing something, I'm sure, but he was inside the parish hall talking to us as we cleaned up after the tea party. Tracy's sister, Ann, who was visiting for the weekend, was also helping tend the church lawn with her family.

"Where else would you see this," we marveled, "except in the country?" We always admire long family chains—probably because our own links to the country are so tenuous and so short.

And now, the California Sisters feel like that mother standing on shore while her sons head for the Promised Land, as Uncle Hank and Aunt Gertie leave Ramona. We don't know how life will go on without them, and yet we are brave, pioneering women and we'll make it.

"We're fast becoming the older generation of Schuberts in Ramona," I say to my sister.

"We knew this day would come," she soothes, "and we've done all the things we wanted to do with them."

She's right. We do have wonderful memories—four years and more, spending another day in the country together.

Tim Steinborn stacking hay on his 115 acre mini-farm east of Ramona. Circa 2002

Haying Time

"Is your Dad baling hay this afternoon?" I asked my young friend Cole.

With a swagger in his step, this country-raised, ten-year-old led me out to the field where he reached under a swath of hay, turned some over, and shook his head. "It's not dry enough, yet," he said with a serious wisdom.

As he stood up and stretched to his full height, the top of his head just matched the height of the uncut hay in the field beside him.

There's so much about haying that I don't know. I didn't know, for instance, that there were several days that usually elapsed between cutting the hay and stacking the hay safely away in the barn—it all depends on the weather. When the magic day arrives and the hay is ready for swathing it either lays in the field where it's cut, or it's raked and turned to dry faster for baling. I had thought it was probably a one-day-deal with all the current automation.

In the days that followed, as we waited for the hay to dry, the bailer to work properly, and helping hands to be available, we all kept an eye on the weather—and this wasn't even my hay!

We sat down to a late supper one night at a friend's house and discovered that our neighbor's had been baling hay until the wee hours of the morning, and they were going back out yet that night, "Once the moisture content gets up a bit," was the comment.

To the novice, it seemed that there were too many things to watch in this farming business—either the moisture was too high or too low, the weather too warm or too cold, the days too short or too long.

The hay in Tooltime Tim's field was being put up in those small traditional old bales. "It's a practice that's dying out," he said. "These days most farmers think it's too much work to make small bales."

Times and practices are always changing. Tim could remember when his Grandpa used to put loose hay up in the barn. "And if it was too green, he'd sprinkle rock salt on the alfalfa to cure it out," said Tim.

Meanwhile back in the field, some of the hay had been baled, and needed to be under cover before our forty percent chance of rain became reality.

As a kid when we'd come back to Ramona for harvest time, I always envied the guys who got to drive the trucks—it looked so exciting to be part of this group effort. Well, I finally got my chance. Tim needed help, and I grabbed my camera to document this phenomena of haying time. "So what's hay season like for you?" I asked, like a true reporter should.

Tired eyes looked at me, and sweat dripped off Tim's face, "At the moment, I'd say it's a lot of damn work, and we aren't even half done." There's a pause as he catches his breath. "If the weather will just cooperate." That seems to be the farmer's prayer. We're either praying for rain or praying for no rain.

With all the automation that was available to cut, rake, bale, clump, clamp, accumulate (I believe, they call it), shift, shove and stack hay, in the end what became most effective was just plain old man power. To save the hay from the threatening weather—it was one man lifting, tossing, pulling, heaving, rearranging bale after bale, until the trailer was full and heading for the barn—and then the process was reversed. On that one trailer alone, there was about six tons of hay. I got weary just watching.

In the days when I owned horses in California, I'd have given my eyeteeth for a trailer load of hay like this, and I felt guilty recalling how I used to fuss at the cost per bale. Now that I've experienced the process at closer range, it seems pretty darn cheap.

It's another day in the country, the hay still isn't all cut, and I notice the wheat is ripening in the fields at a pretty fast clip. In every single season there's more than just one reason to be worried about the weather.

These kids are cherished "move-ins" and hold the future of Ramona in their hands: Terren Thompson, Josh and Molly Mercer and Cassy Thompson.
Circa 2004

Mayberry, R.F.D.

There's always a breeze blowing through Ramona. When it comes from the south, it's warm. When it blows from the north, cool air rides the current.

According to Aunt Gertie, the weather prophet, "Trouble comes out of the west."

"It's the southwest," Uncle Hank adds.

People seem to blow through a small town just like that Kansas wind, tumbling before the forces of nature like pop cans thoughtlessly tossed from a passing car window or skittering in the breeze like yesterday's advertisement brochure. They are snagged in town for a day, a week, a month or maybe even a school year in an empty trailer house or on a friend's living room floor. And then they are gone, and we don't even know who picked them up!

The old-timers in town hold their breath when a house comes up empty next door. "Who will move in?" they wonder. They hope the "move-ins" will be a nice young couple with clean, well-disciplined children or a retired couple willing to be involved in the Senior Center, or a family with relatives in the area.

We're always pleased when the new folk come by and introduce themselves like Jim did a week or so ago, fresh from the city. "This is my wife Terri, my mother Joyce, and Ben, Terren, Dallen, Cassy and CJ," he said, proudly introducing his kids.

How pleased we were to meet this passel of politely curious children. "I brought my family here from California in hopes of experiencing Mayberry, R.F.D.," Jim added with a chuckle.

Since we experienced Ramona long before Mayberry was a TV show, I had never thought of this town as "the Mayberry experience." But it could be!

In the fictional Mayberry everybody knows your name and your business, there's help available at the drop of a hat, the streets are safe, and you can trust your neighbor. Town folk watch your children grow up, correct them if they need it, are supportive and kind. They may even attend school functions long after their own kids are grown. Family names are familiar, everybody is a relative in one way or another, the church communities set a healthy tone in town, and problems get resolved within the hour. If only it was as easy as Aunt Bea and Andy made it seem!

My sister and I often wonder what really binds folks together besides family ties. Where's the "Director," and what happens when your neighbor's dogs are loose and characters don't follow the "script"?

A Mayberry, R.F.D. experience doesn't just happen. Nor is it unattainable. You've got to work at it as diligently as you weed your garden, mow your lawn, corral your pooch, and pay your bills. It's a mind-set, a commitment to the Golden Rule—a worthy goal for any small town.

While bad things happen—folks are disappointed and sometimes get a little miffed at one another—we try to stay optimistic in Ramona. Certainly those Girls from California are determined to keep talking about the good stuff! "Look on the bright side," we remind ourselves. "Remember why we're here!"

Some days we get discouraged and wonder if the dream is reachable. "How did you make it growing up in Ramona?" we ask Tooltime Tim.

"Ah, you just don't expect too much," he answers, knowing full well that we're really in trouble on that count. We have high expectations!

It's another day in the country, and I have high hopes for Ramona, that's for sure. We've had a few temporary "move-ins" blow through town but, hey, we've been here for three years! And, we've experienced at least a twenty percent increase in our community this past year. Praise be for the solid old-timers who've kept Ramona viable all these years, and Heaven bless the "move-ins" as we work to create Mayberry R.F.D. on the Kansas prairie!

Nothing more beautiful than a sunset on the plains of Kansas. Circa 2001

A Country Send-Off

This place, the Midwest, the Heartland, has got to be the best place in the world to die—although people don't really use the word *die*. They say things like *passed on*, *deceased*, or *gone*!

When my sister and I first started coming to Ramona for summer vacation we always noticed when there was a funeral procession—all the cars washed, with their lights on, and all the men in suits. It's heart-warming to behold.

And then one Saturday we met an entourage of cars with their headlights on, everyone dressed up, and we slowed our pace out of respect. "Look at that," said my sister. "They've even fastened little purple flags on all the cars. Isn't that nice." (Later on we discovered this was *not* a funeral procession, but a group of football fans heading toward Manhattan for a K-State game.)

Whenever I go to the grocery store, I see the notices of funerals and memorial services laying on the checkout counter. I always stop and read these notices; I'm curious as to how long the deceased enjoyed life, and I wonder if they ever had any connection to my family.

Let me assure you, there are no notices about funerals on grocery store checkout stands in California. There, you read the obituary column of the newspaper, and if you aren't prompt, or had a busy season, you wouldn't find out someone had died until long past any memorials.

In a small town people know if you're sick, if you fell down in the parking lot, or if you've *passed on*, and they are right there at your door with a casserole dish. A small community keeps track of calamities. In the city, however, you could be out of commission for months and no one would know the difference—unless your newspapers started stacking up outside your front door.

A few years back we were getting ready to leave for the summer, and return to California, and were all set to make our rounds—saying good bye to family and friends. (This always took us at least an hour.)

"We'll come by around nine to tell you good-bye," we told Tony Meyer, who lives just down the street.

"You'd better come before then," he countered, "because Erich and I are going to a funeral over in Hope."

"What time is the service?" I wanted to know.

"It's at 10:30," came the reply.

"It only takes ten minutes to get to Hope, and you're leaving at nine o'clock?"

"We've got to get a good seat," he said. "If you're going to a funeral you want to be able to sit down, and you want to be able to hear—so you'd better be there early! These Kansas funerals are often overcrowded."

That was the year we went to see Leon Bura, who was then secretary-treasurer of the Cemetery Committee, and bought ourselves grave plots in Lewis Cemetery. I was finally taking Uncle Hank's advice.

My aunts remind me, some coming from as far away as Wichita for funerals in this area, "This is when we get to see all of our cousins." And relatively speaking, there's a lot of connecting during this important ritual. Funerals are a real get-together in the country—not just a fly-by. The community turns out in full force.

When Sean Bailey died about a year ago, I experienced this mid-western funeral phenomena first hand. Sean was my neighbor and a pretty quiet guy—other than with family and close friends. When we joined his funeral entourage—which was over a mile long, with more flashing lights than I'd ever seen in San Francisco—I said to my sister, "Sean would have gotten a hoot out of this!" His friends made sure that he got his due.

Well, it's another day in the country and while I believe in living every day to its fullest, if you want to be remembered with an overflow crowd and sirens, the best place of all to meet your Maker is in the country!

This huge cedar tree went down in Erich's yard illustrating the saying, "The wind prunes the trees and time the populace." Circa 1994

The Old Timers

One by one, the old timers are leaving Ramona. As I walked to our office in the old bank building, I was wondering about the definition of an old timer. It probably means someone in their eighties. Most likely, it's someone who has lived here in Ramona for a long, long time.

Bert Schneider was an old timer in Ramona. She ran the grocery store in town for many years until 1988. After that, she lived quietly in her house on C Street, until she had a stroke and needed additional care. She died last year and her funeral was a small one because her contemporaries are mostly all gone—her era, fast fading into history.

It's my mother's era. At 88, Mom lives in an age of push buttons and computers—nothing is simple. She's lucky to have four of her eight siblings still alive. And still sometimes she says, "It's time for me to get off the planet—the world is changing too fast." Sometimes it is no fun being an old timer.

Hank and Gertie Schubert did an exodus on Memorial Weekend when their children took them to Colorado. Another set of old timers exiting Stage Right. At least we can still talk to them on the phone. But it's not the same in Ramona without them. Our aunt and uncle were town fixtures—someone who'd been here forever. And now I mention their names to keep them alive in our memories.

Tony Meyer is one of our old timers, the oldest in town—although when I ask him for specifics on stories, he'd usually say to me, "Talk to Erich! He's got the good memory." It used to be that when I stopped by Tony's house in the afternoon, the two would be taking a break from farming, and be snoozing or watching TV.

Over Fourth of July weekend I saw Erich Utech—a long-time stalwart in Ramona, who recently moved to a care facility when his health took a turn. He was briefly in town to watch the parade and see his friends and family.

Erich had a feeling his time on earth was coming to a close, and in November 2004 his spirit departed. Erich now rests in Lewis Cemetery.

On the day of Erich's funeral it rained something fierce. So intense was the storm that the electricity went out in the church where his funeral was held. I smiled, because Erich always loved to tell "weather stories," and now we had one to add to the collection. Pastor Davis commented that he'd heard of candlelight suppers, but never a candlelight funeral, until now.

Even though Tony routinely says, "What am I gonna do now that Erich is not here—rot in Ramona?" we know Tony, and we know he'll not rot. His restless nature keeps things stirred up.

One minute he's calling to elicit my help on an advertising campaign, and the next he's got a dinner party cooked up. "I'm taking six women to dinner," he declares. "Do you think I can handle it?" and then he chuckles with delight.

Jakie Brunner was another Ramona old timer and he, too, is long gone. His door was one we always knocked on when we'd come back to Ramona in the summer. We wondered if he'd be there when we returned, year after year. "I'll probably be out there with Momma," he'd say to us, motioning to the cemetery. "Now don't you *sweethearts* forget to pick those peonies."

This year was not particularly good peony weather. I guiltily looked at the weeds in Jake's peony patch and said, "I've got to get these out of here before Memorial Day—Jake would be mortified to see weeds in his flower beds."

Jess took a bunch of his flowers out to the cemetery with a note, "To the Peony King." (And yes, I'd gotten the weeds out beforehand).

Today I have bills to pay and lawns to mow, flower beds to weed and a bed of my own to make—but I must take time to say how important you old timers are to all of us! You are the rock upon which we stand, as we build the future on another day in the country.

During planting or harvest, farmers often work late into the night. Circa 2002

Life's Final Act

It certainly wasn't my father's idea to come back to Kansas to spend another day in the country. He was already living out his country-living dream on a little acreage in Oregon. "Why would you want to go back to Ramona," he'd say, "when I worked so hard to get out of there?"

But it was plain to see that our parents needed to be living near us and guess where we were? Ramona. To some degree Dad came to terms with this—once he was here. His health was critical and he spent many hours sitting on the edge of his bed looking out the window on once familiar territory. He watched Ralph drive off to get his mail. He watched his sister, Naomi, step to the door to retrieve her newspaper. He watched the Hares putting up their Christmas decorations.

One day he said, "I've been thinking about all the people I've known here in Ramona—good people, salt-of-the-earth people," and he proceeded to name the family names that are so familiar to us all in this part of the country. He had tears in his eyes as he recited the list of people.

Another day he said, "When I'm here in Ramona I half expect to see my Dad. This is where he always was and I feel that any minute he'll come to the door. It seems so strange that he's not here."

When I repeated this to Aunt Naomi, she said, "It gives me a funny feeling to hear him say that—as if he's expecting to die." And he was.

Five years ago, the doctors had told him to get his house in order. But, Dad had so many near-death experiences—where one minute we'd be planning his funeral and the next minute he'd be up trying to build a house—that my sister said she was going to call him "Lazarus."

And then this morning Dad died. By the time he took his final breath, we were relieved that he had been released from his suffering. On the way back from the hospital in the black of a prairie night, I thought of all those who had gone before.

My grandfather, Solomon Ehrhardt, died on the job. Grandpa died helping a friend lay brick. Dad would have liked to have had his life come to an end in that fashion—unexpected, doing something he loved. He would

have liked to have been driving his tractor or walking on his land when he died. Instead he lingered and struggled in a hospital bed.

My grandmother, Auguste Bentz Schubert died when she was cleaning out the china cabinet. The day grandma died, is indelibly imprinted on Uncle Hank's memory. "Olga Schneider was the telephone operator and she called me in Herington at work and told me that my dad had called a doctor and she said she thought I'd better come home," said Hank. Her death was a surprise to her family and to her—she had potatoes peeled for dinner setting in the kitchen.

We retell the family stories around death and dying at a time like this—how Grandma Ehrhardt, in a coma, raised her eyebrows when she heard Aunt Naomi's voice, how Uncle Kenneth went so quickly on a cold winter day.

My Dad loved to tell the story of his grandmother's death. "The whole family had gathered at Grandma's bedside and while the adults stood watch, we kids scampered around the yard, in and out of the house," Dad recalled. "One of my aunts was called the crying aunt because she carried on so at funerals, and she was kneeling close to the head of the bed, intently watching her mother for signs of life. Suddenly, my grandma took a deep gasping breath, exhaled and lay very still. The family assumed it was her last breath and the crying aunt started wailing, whereupon Grandma Glantz opened her eyes and said, 'Did you think I was dead?' And then she died!" Dad loved this story.

As we stood at Dad's bedside and he struggled to talk, I was reminded that whatever needs to be said should be said today! Life is a strange and wonderful gift and death is part of the package.

Today, as I spend another day in the country, I'll rejoice in life. Maybe I'll get Dad's tractor out and go for a spin!

One of Jakie's peonies drenched with spring rain—I've taken pictures of hundreds of them. Just can't resist. Circa 1995

Remembering to Remember

Coming from California, where the majority of the people are transplants from other places, I'm not used to seeing the generational procession to the graveyard that I always witness in Ramona on Memorial weekend. No loved ones of mine are buried in California soil. I had no graves to decorate.

In Kansas, however, my cousins always return to Lewis Cemetery—it's a yearly quest. They often stop for a chat on the porch, so we get the benefit of touching bases.

Joe comes prepared with a shovel for digging plants into the ground, Georgia arrives with silk flowers and name tags stating "Mother" and "Father."

Glenn and Lois bring wire flower holders that keep their artificial flower gift from tumbling off into the sunset, in front of our perpetual Kansas wind.

There's a longing to return—some satisfaction in remembering. My mother once brought flowers and greenery clear from her garden in Oregon to make bouquets to decorate her parents' grave here in Kansas.

"I get to do it so seldom," she said explaining her heroics.

Rituals are soothing. There's something comforting about seeing these yearly tasks performed. I wonder if the family members talk about the people whose grave they are decorating. Does the grandma tell the children about the man who once was her mate? Does the mother laugh and tell stories about her parents and her siblings when they were small? I hope so!

Whenever we came to Kansas—no matter the season—my sister would go out to the cemetery on her first early-morning walk to "check on the relatives." (This, of course, occurs after we've informed those *living* in town that we're back).

As we become the older generation, the mantel of remembering settles on our shoulders. We consider it our job to repeat the family stories to the children, and we make it a priority to reflect our ancestors on the walls of every home we own.

Early Monday morning on Memorial Day we were at our friend Jakie's grave, giving him some of his precious peonies. Because spring came early this year, I had to save peony buds in the refrigerator per all of Jakie's previous instructions.

Little did we know when he'd instruct us to "pick arm's full of them peonies when you come back in the spring, Sveetharts—I'll tell my boy Donny," that some day we'd own his home.

"And where will you be when we return?" we'd ask Jake. "Ahhh, out there in the cemetery with Momma," he'd answer as he pointed southwest.

As we deliver our flowers to family graves, a long-legged boy strides across the carefully mowed lawn with flowers in his hand to put on a grave. I don't know him.

An unfamiliar car drives slowly past—they seem to be checking on things.

Someone on a Harley motorcycle drives in and stops for a few minutes at a grave on the west side. It's Jim and he's been at his father's grave. He waves as he rides out of the cemetery.

There's something very touching about this early-morning procession. There's camaraderie in remembering—we're all in this together.

It doesn't really make much difference if our presentation is "too showy," as my aunt says, or "not showy enough." It doesn't really matter—except for conversational purposes—whether we've erected a shrine to honor our loved ones or just left a single blossom.

It's another day in the country, the meadowlarks are singing, flags are snapping in the breeze, taps has been played, and we're alive and well, standing side by side with family and friends on Memorial Day—remembering.

When the train is across the tracks in Ramona, as it often is, we say, "The iron curtain is down." Circa 2000

Clickity Clack

You've got to cross the railroad tracks to even get into my little town. With only 5 blocks going in any direction you never get very far away from the tracks or the sound of the trains.

On the telephone the other day the train whistle momentarily overwhelmed my voice. "Boy, you must live close to the tracks," my caller said. To a city dweller, a tiny town like Ramona is hard to imagine.

The sound of the train coming clickity clack along the tracks, or the whistle blowing into the wind, is oddly comforting to me, because it is one of my earliest childhood memories. Now, as I lay curled up on my feather bed at night with the sweet summer breeze blowing through the room, I stretch my ears to hear the first calls in the distance and smile when I hear them.

My grandpa Ehrhardt, working in the field west of town, would always pause when the train went by—almost out of respect. "Whoa," he'd say to the team of horses. "Whoa there, Jim. Here it comes." He'd take a deep breath, pull out his red handkerchief, take off his cap and wipe his sweaty brow.

"It must be around 4 o'clock," he'd announce to no one in particular. The Rock Island Line, dissecting his land and regulating his life, was as good as a clock on the wall.

When Grandma and Grandpa Schubert moved to town, we cousins would race down to the crossing by the co-op to welcome the train, wave it on by, and thrill if the engineer tooted the whistle at us. We'd sneak pennies onto the tracks ahead of time and collect their flattened shapes later on. We'd count the number of cars and compare, "How many did you get?" Children's fascination with trains is legendary in these parts.

My friend Tony, now 93, remembers the day he and two of his brothers ran away from home to see the California Zephyr.

They'd heard grown-ups talking about the magnificence of that train and these three little country kids—five, six and seven—wanted to see it for themselves. So, when their Mama wasn't looking they took off down the road, across the fields, to wait for that wonderful train to come huffing and puffing down the tracks from Herington.

"What a sight it was," Tony recalls, "they were really pouring on the coal to that old steam engine. It was blowing black smoke up into the sky and we three kids were so intimidated that we hid in the wheat field beside the tracks as the train went by. We didn't even have the nerve to stand up and wave."

Three little boys marveling at the power that made the ground shake and the air tremble. Can't you just see them peering through the tall Kansas wheat with wide eyes?

"Of course," Tony continues, "when we got home, Mama had the peach tree branches all ready for us, and she beat the hell out of us for running away!"

"Was it worth it?" I wanted to know.

"It sure was," and Tony laughs at the memory, "I'd do it again any day!"

As I walk home from Tony's house, I can hear a train in the distance warning of its approach.

"Here it comes," I catch myself saying to no one in particular. "Must be around 4 o'clock," on another day in the country.

Schubert cousins—Keith, Alan, Gary, Jess and Pat—enjoying the nostalgic atmosphere of Betty's Restaurant which closed in 2000. Circa 1986

A Passel of Cousins

I remember walking through my aunt Anna's pasture one summer afternoon with a passel of cousins. We'd come back to Ramona for a family reunion and had been invited out to Anna's for a potluck supper.

This land was familiar terrain for all of us. We knew which way to look in order to see the outcropping of trees where Grandma Schubert's house used to be. We knew the sound of the wind whistling around the eaves in Anna's attic. As children we'd played in the hayloft of the barn and watched the barn swallows sweep in and out of the windows. We remembered the sound of Uncle Walter's voice and the way he dipped his head when he chuckled and swiped his hand across his hair. These memories bound us together as we walked in the field that summer afternoon.

But we weren't children any longer; years had flown by since we'd played together. How were we going to get reacquainted? How could we say anything meaningful to one another after the many years of accumulated life experiences?

"How about let's tell each other some event that shaped our lives," I suggested.

"How about telling the most difficult experience you've had so far?" my sister chimed in, upping the ante. "I'll go first," she said and bravely forged ahead telling a story to this group of relative strangers—a story no one had heard before.

We just kept walking in the field, our hands absentmindedly sweeping the tall grass. Sometimes we stopped and made eye contact. A couple of times we hugged one another. Mostly we just meandered and listened to each other. A hand would reach out and touch another hand and squeeze. We'd smile into a familiar face that we'd first encountered when it was chubby-cheeked and very young—and here we were, older and wiser, walking together in Aunt Anna's pasture.

When we headed back toward the house, something had changed. There had been a shift in our relativity. You could feel it in the air. There was a sense of cousin camaraderie and the aunts and uncles sitting on the porch and standing around in the shade felt it.

"What have you kids been doing?" Aunt Gertie called.

"What have you guys been talking about for so long out there?" Uncle Clarence wanted to know.

"We've been telling our most difficult life experiences," one cousin answered. And one uncle said, "What were they?"

"In order to hear the stories, you have to be willing to tell yours. Do you want to join us?" we replied. Everyone stayed put except for one. One brave uncle joined us as we trouped into Aunt Anna's cool kitchen for a drink. One uncle told his story as we stood in a circle listening.

It was Anna's youngest brother, sweet spirited Arthur, telling about being on a submarine during World War II. We'd all seen Uncle Art's photograph—dressed up in his Navy uniform—setting on Grandma's sideboard but we'd never heard this story. He told about being on a sub one night out on patrol, ordered not to defend themselves, sitting ducks just waiting for one depth charge to get close enough, for one torpedo to hit its mark. While he was in American water on maneuvers, German subs had also been reported in the area. He was scared. He told us about standing on the conning tower the next morning, watching the sun rise, with the realization that he was miraculously alive.

We all bunched together and hugged this uncle of ours, who had tears in his eyes, rejoicing that he was with us, and brave enough to join our circle. It was one of the last times we had together with him.

That walk in the pasture, listening to the collection of stories told by childhood playmates, now grown, was the catalyst that continues to bring us back year after year to Ramona for our Schubert family reunions.

It's another day in the country and our houses are very quiet. The last of the cousins and their kids finally drove out of Ramona. Waving them on their way, we marvel at the turn of events that leaves us planted in this place that our cousins all left behind.

A wagon full of produce from our garden to pull around town and offer to our relatives and neighbors. Betty said, "Are you trying to put me out of business?" Circa 2003

Star Gardeners

There are several star-gardeners in Ramona. I think Kink Sondergard won the honors this year for having the first peas. His garden is a wonder to behold—always completely weed-free.

Betty Ohm takes the prize for being our town's most prolific gardener. She grows everything and does it well! She is our standard of measurement in the community.

"Has Betty planted her potatoes? Well, then, we'd better get ours in," we say. And if you can get something up in your garden before Betty, you've accomplished something because this lady starts early!

A couple of summers ago, my uncle Hank—whose garden consisted of one very gigantic, well-tended, tomato plant—was so proud of the fact that he was able to pick a beautiful prize tomato *before* Betty. Of course, he had to go show it off to her. We even documented the event with a picture.

This town is a little like Betty's garden. It's lined up and ordered in straight rows along the street.

Some of us growing here are from old familiar seed, like Burpee's Big Boy. Others have mixed heritage, coming up topsy-turvy from a tomato thrown out beside the road somewhere—not even knowing their brand name—just struggling to survive, transplanted in and still reeling from the shock. Some have taken off and grown like dandelions, needing only a scrap of soil and sunshine to multiply and divide. Others are frail and tentative, not sure if they belong.

We've always admired those sturdy blooms in Ramona that come from native stock, like our friend Tooltime Tim who has grown up here and thrives. By contrast, coming from California we feel more like hothouse tomatoes, sheltered and pampered, accustomed to fine soil and weekly fertilizer.

When we came to Ramona just for the summer, we carried our city life around with us, like a potted container, that we could jump back into at any moment. Ramona was an adventure. Country life was just an interesting possibility.

I remember the days when we worked in a California office building and tantalized ourselves with the idea of planting our feet in Kansas for a season, saying, "What if?" We'd heard stories about how tough you had to be to survive in Kansas, where the wind blows almost every day, and it can go ninety days without rain, and not even break a record. We wondered if we'd ever survive in this environment.

The first summer we were in Kansas, Kink and Darlene brought by garden produce on a regular basis, "If we keep bringing you something to eat, will you stay?" Darlene wanted to know.

Our own little patch of vegetables had gotten a late start but thanks to David's rototilling and Clinton's chicken manure, it literally jumped up out of the ground!

This spring, A.J. brought more fertilizer from his mini-farm and we got our garden planted "on time," as they say. And we're enjoying the fruits of our labor.

We had our first "garden dinner" a couple of weeks ago with everything on the table coming from our vegetable patch: new potatoes and peas, cabbage, beets, green onions. The cukes are setting on like gangbusters and I picked my first tomatoes this week, and let them finish ripening on the kitchen windowsill.

The neighbor's gardens are growing, too. Yesterday I received two surprise packages on my front porch—zucchini donations.

It's another day and in the country we're not just surviving, but thriving—with a little help from our friends.

Tooltime Tim, left, was buying an ancient corn planter from Lawrence Svoboda when, in a junk pile, he spied an old Maytag for our museum. Circa 2003

Save That

There is something frugal in my genetic make-up that has come down through the generations. I save things that ordinary people would throw away.

For instance, I save scraps of old partially used candles to re-melt and dip into lovely tapers. I don't know that my grandmother ever made candles, but she did save the paraffin off the top of jelly jars to re-melt and seal next year's jam.

Grandma always made soap from the lard and grease drippings that she carefully saved. She saved flour sacks and traded them with her friends to make dresses. She saved scraps of cloth and worn out clothes to make quilts. She saved feathers from chickens and geese and made pillows and feather ticks.

I save feathers from dead birds that the cats drag onto the porch. I save perfect cornhusks, bits of leather from old worn out boots and horsehair. I save beads and tiny buttons. These things eventually turn into lovely cornhusk Indian dolls.

There is an uncommon joy that springs up when you make something out of nothing. Ok, it isn't *nothing*—it's just something someone else might have thrown away.

For example, folks out in the country tend to save defunct farm equipment, rather than dispose of it. Drive down country roads near Ramona and you'll see tractors nestled in the weeds, old trucks stranded in the field, and worn out implements stashed behind a barn.

This is perplexing to our mother, who likes to see a tidy landscape. "Why don't they just get rid of that junk?" Mom wonders.

"I've got three old trucks in my yard," answered Tooltime Tim, "and they're worth more to me than if I sold 'em. Never know when I might need a part off one of those trucks to fix something else!"

Sometimes this habit of saving gets to be an annoyance—especially to the souls who live with you! It also can be a personal burden, because I can see a future use for almost anything—including road kill.

This skill of seeing the potential in discards is akin to the country skill of making-do. I'm good at this, too. Perhaps it comes from a long line of ancestors who honed the talent.

I believe you need to have a penchant for country living in order to do this innately. My sister, born and bred in the city doesn't have it. She's more like Dad (who ruins my theory since *he* was raised on a farm). She likes new fresh things, preferably store bought. Throw it away is her motto. "If you can't use it now, get rid of it," she chants as she views the over-stuffed fridge.

Inspiration comes from cleaning the refrigerator—which I don't do often enough, according to my sis. "Just give me a day or two!" I counter. That broccoli I saved becomes yummy broccoli soup, if I can salvage it before Jess tosses it out. Old tortillas and cheese that is threatening to mold, turn into enchiladas with the addition of a delicious make-do sauce made out of tomato paste and saved salsa. Scraps of cooked vegetables become minestrone with the addition of a hand full of pasta and the right seasoning.

Mom saves potato water, which most folks pour down the drain, for gravy or soup stock. She saves cream that has turned sour for any number of delicious causes, and left-over mashed potatoes become the best bread in the world!

It's another day in the country and, as a matter of fact, today is the day Mom bakes bread—can you smell it? I bet if we could just *save that* smell, we could sell it!

This windmill is all that remains at the home site where my parents farmed on a Scully lease southwest of Ramona. Circa 2004

Good Ole' Country Wisdom

We've been in the country now almost a thousand days and I'm still confounded by the ways of Kansas weather! Try as I might to figure out the whims of a season, something always trips me up.

Last spring, I heard the adage, "You should plant your potatoes by St. Patrick's Day," and I did. Wouldn't you know it, we had a late frost and my little baby potato plants all got nipped rather severely and never quite recovered their vigor!

Not to be deterred, I tried it again this year—and so far so good—but some folks in town are already on their second planting of potatoes.

I even went so far as to purchase a Farmer's Almanac and the first prediction that I came across said that we were going to have an extremely wet year—starting in January. So, I was mentally prepared for a wet and soggy spring—we haven't had one! I lost faith in the Almanac.

Always on the lookout for a hot tip or getting a leg up on the learning curve, I've been listening to old timers.

So far, I've learned how to cure warts. "Steal a dish cloth, rub it on your wart and bury the cloth," I was told. "By the time the dish cloth rots, the wart will be gone." I was rightly skeptical. "It works," I was told.

"How long does it take a dish cloth to rot?" I wanted to know.

"A while," came the sage reply.

I figure that if you want to be done with a wart in a hurry, you'd better steal an old and rather rotten dish cloth in the first place which will serve you well on both ends—with whomever you stole it from, and God.

I've received lots of advice about when the frost is coming in the fall, which I'll have to remember. "When you hear the katy-dids sing, frost is six weeks away." Does anyone know what a katy-did sounds like?

Or "When you see the first wild asters blooming—then frost is six weeks away." As for frost in the spring, they told me that when the hedge tree leaves are the size of the ear of a mouse, you'll have the last frost.

They also told me—these wise and witty country sages—that I plant my corn when the hedge leaves are as big as a squirrel's ear. I see that I'm going to have to brush up on anatomy. Anyone measured a squirrel's ear lately?

Meanwhile I've also received tips about what you do when someone gives you the start of a plant. "Don't ever thank them," Mary Alice told me, "or your plant won't grow."

Probably the most catchy information I've received was for fishermen—alas, I don't fish.

You can almost sing this ditty. "When the wind's in the west, the fishing is best," Doris said. "When the wind's in the east your catch is the least. When the wind's in the north—do not go forth. And when the wind's in the south it blows the bait to the fishes' mouth."

The country wisdom continues, "Don't plant in any month with an *R* in the name."

Immediately, they were contradicted. "No, you can only eat rabbits in a month with an *R* in the name."

I just opted out of that conversation—it was too confusing, and furthermore I don't eat rabbits.

I've been hankering for a big plot of corn so Tooltime Tim told me that I could use his corral for a corn patch, and we've been tilling it up in anticipation of planting corn.

Thinking I'd gotten the hang of this country thing I told Tim, "Can't we plant that corn now? The leaves of David's red bud tree are now the size of a squirrel's ear."

"Nah," he said. "*That's* when you are supposed to go hunting for mushrooms. You can't plant corn until the *hedge* leaves are that big."

Ah, well, it's another day in the country, and I feel like a babe in the woods when it comes to country wisdom.

Our very own garden corn, five minutes from the stalk to the table. Can't you just taste it? Circa 2003

Corn Country

Corn has always been an important part of our diet, whether we were in the country or city-dwellers. Because we're a gardening family, we know the difference, too, between store-bought corn and corn lovingly frozen ourselves and stored in the freezer. We know the difference between corn that comes fresh from the garden and directly into a steaming kettle of hot water and corn that is picked, shipped, doused with chemicals to keep it semi-fresh and refrigerated until finally it appears in the local grocery. There is no comparison!

And even though we are amazed at corn appearing in the grocery store in February, we know that it comes from Mexico or El Salvador and has experienced a long and arduous journey. No way are we even tempted to buy it and put it on our table.

Even with all the genetic manipulations to make corn sweeter and sweeter, so that we are tricked into believing it is fresh when it isn't, we (who have farmer's blood in our veins) know the difference!

Of course, coming to Kansas corn-country, immediately our hearts turned toward homegrown corn and the delicious treat of taking corn straight from the garden and into our mouths in five minutes or less (which includes shucking time). Mmmm, good!

However, lately, it just seemed that my little backyard garden couldn't support enough corn to even whet our appetite. My heart yearned for more! Enter Tooltime Tim on his white horse. "So how much corn do you want to plant?" he asked.

"Lots!" came the answer.

He pondered my response a minute and then said, "Next year, we'll plow up my corral and you can plant corn up there!"

Well, next year is here! "How much more do you want tilled up?" Tim hollered as he plowed back and forth.

"More!" I yelled. When we were finally finished, I looked at this field we'd groomed for corn. It was huge!

"This is how it works," Tim made it clear. "I'll get it ready. You take care of it!" A deal was a deal.

We found an old two-row planter out at Svoboda's farm, brought it home, hooked it up behind Dad's John Deere and triumphantly planted the first ten rows of corn.

We waited. No sprouts appeared. We hadn't set the planter correctly, so we tried again. What a triumphant day when that corn came up! Of course, so did the weeds.

Jessica and I have been out hoeing in that field. As we chop we remember stories Mom told about hoeing weeds with her siblings on a hot summer day.

"We got smart and hooked up the horse and buggy. We took turns sitting in back and chopping until the hoe got caught in the buggy wheel," Mom laughed. "Then we were back to walking."

"Now, we need a two-row cultivator," the toolman proclaimed. We're still looking for one.

"How much are you going to invest in this corn before it ever hits the plate?" my sister wanted to know. She thinks we'd be better off going to Lehigh and buying our corn from Ted McIrvin. "He's got rows and rows of beautiful corn," she chides.

But, we'll keep trying. It's another day in the country and surely growing your own corn is a country tradition worth keeping!

Jakie Brunner waves from his vintage Chevrolet as he cruises the streets of town on his way home from the Post office. Circa 1990

The Kansas Wave

One of the cultural differences we noted when we came from California to Kansas was that everyone in Kansas seemed to wave. By contrast, a *wave* in California is something you do at a sporting event, or catch on your surfboard at the beach.

The first time someone waved at us my sister looked at me and asked, "Do we *know* those people?"

Waving was a mid-western phenomena. Someone passing as you crossed the street called forth a wave. Meeting in cars on a dirt road caused folks to wave. Even on the highway—where traffic was relatively busy—people waved. We were experiencing culture shock.

"We'd better wave, too," I said to my sister. "It's the custom."

Since everyone waved in Ramona we bowed to the rule, but we had to practice. After careful observation we discovered different styles of waving. There was the head nod, the one-finger-raised-from-the-top-of-the-steering-wheel wave, the two-fingered-semi-salute wave, the simple hand wave, and the exuberant arm-out-the-window wave. We weren't quite sure which one to choose.

"And if you don't wave, people will think you are rude or mad at them," said our friend Tooltime Tim. "Nothing more disgusting than when you drive by and someone just looks and looks at you and doesn't wave. So *wave!*" he said, "even if you don't know 'em."

We could see we'd better stop staring and start waving. Whether or not we were engrossed in mowing the lawn, we waved at the people driving by to check on our progress. No matter if we were in deep conversation driving down the road with kids in the back seat misbehaving, we practiced smiling and waving at those we met on the road.

"There *is* a limit to this waving thing," Aunt Naomi said. She once had a neighbor who was constantly driving in and out of his drive way, and every time he drove past her house he'd wave—ten, fifteen times a day.

"Enough is enough," she grumbled. "I'll wave once or twice a day to the same person and that's it. They can think I'm unfriendly, but I'm worn out from waving."

As I contemplated this waving thing, I remembered the first summer we were here in Kansas. Just beginning to get the hang of this waving business, we were trying to remember our manners and we waved at each car that we passed. We waved to people walking along the road and farmers out on their tractors in the field.

And then one day as we were driving out of town we spied someone in the distance combining wheat. It was Mr. Wingerd and he was approaching the corner of his field at about the same pace as we were approaching the bend in the road that adjoined his land. We were going to meet him at the corner and immediately we were in a waving dilemma.

My sister and I looked at each other, "Do you think we should wave?" we wanted to know—not wanting to offend someone we'd just met.

"But is it safe?" After all, Dale only had one arm and that arm was most surely needed on the controls of the combine.

Our eyes got bigger as we approached the corner. My two hands gripped the steering wheel and my sister sat on hers. Should we pretend we didn't see him for his own good?

Never fear, he saw us! As he turned the corner his arm flew out the window of the combine with the biggest friendliest Kansas wave we'd ever seen.

"Whew! Imagine that—waving while driving a combine and turning a corner in a bumpy wheat field so close to the barbed wire fence. And he did it all with only one arm!" We decided that waving must be really important around here!

It's many years later and another day in the country. I finally called Dale Wingerd and asked, "So, how did you maneuver that corner while waving?"

After he got through laughing, he said, "I just used my knee."

Too few working windmills dot the Kansas skyline. They were once the prairie's most picturesque landmark. Circa 2004

Got Rain?

On Sunday, it rained in Ramona. This rain was indeed noteworthy! What has it been, two months since it rained? I do recall that during the haying season we were praying, "Please, no rain, " but once the wheat was all in, we switched our plea. "Did we say no rain? Well, now we'd like a little."

In California, the Almighty doesn't have to worry about prayer requests for "rain" or "no rain" all summer long. There are probably just too many people with counter requests so the rhythm of nature in the Napa Valley is set to "no rain" from May to September. Every day is filled with consistent sunshine. We know that if you want rain in the summer in California, you've got to turn on the sprinkler system and make your own.

This summer, as things got dry in my Kansas yard, I started watering. It's one thing to be hot yourself, but it's quite another for the gardener to look out and see her tomatoes thirsty.

"You've been squirting again," said our buddy, Tooltime Tim. "You're spoiling them things," he warned. But I can't stand for plants to be all droopy.

"How do you take watching your crops dry up?" I ask my neighbor Erich.

"Oh, we've been through this lots of times before," he chuckles at my concern. "This is nothing," he tells me with a shake of his head. "Why in 1936—now that was the grand daddy of them all." And then he tells me how many days the weather was in the "triple digits" all in a row, setting a Kansas state record. There was no rain, period, until September when it was too late for any crops to be saved.

Every morning during my 2002 mini-drought, I gave thanks for our well. When the pump went kaput, I switched my allegiance and spirit of thanksgiving to Rural Water District #1.

I remember the stories about Grandma getting up early in the morning to carry water to her garden from the pump—every ounce of water pulled up out of the earth in order to replenish the earth.

Through these hot days of a summer my flowers have survived, but they haven't flourished—the same with the milo and the corn in the fields near town.

Instead of reaching towards my shoulders, the zinnias at our Jake's Place guesthouse are down around my knees and blooming fast as if to say, "Quick! Bloom and make seed for the next year, because we don't know how long we'll be alive!"

Several times we thought that rain was coming this summer, and watched the sky and the clouds with great expectations; but nothing happened. We had wind, sometimes thunder and even a little lightening in the area—no rain!

In the midst of all this dryness and heat, I took to even watering the lawn in front of the house. After all, the little strip of land where the flowers lived was instantly sucked dry.

How could anything survive? The terra firma outside my little band of green has cracks in it so large one could lose a small tool to the depths. As the cracks in the ground widened, I wondered if I should just drop something into their gapping mouths—as if to appease the underground gods.

If nothing else, it could tell some distant posterity about our way of life, should they uncover it. "Let them try and figure out how a screwdriver got down there," I chuckled to myself like a mad scientist. (This is what happens when it gets too hot in Kansas and there's no rain.)

And then it rained on Saturday! We were sitting on the porch in the intense heat, shooing the flies, when the wind came up.

"What is this shift in the weather?" I asked no one in particular.

"Was there a forecast for rain?" And the answer came in the wind as big drops of water catapulted to the thirsty ground.

"Did we leave the car windows open?"

The rain was so delicious that I didn't run to close the window—I sauntered, raising my arms to the heavens in thanksgiving for the rain descending.

This was like standing in the shower—the water was so warm. By the time I got back to the house, I was deliciously drenched, and stood at the edge of the porch and let the run-off from the roof just pour over my head. Praise be! It's another day in the country and we got rain!

From upper left and clockwise, the events in town that relieve the monotony: Tooltime Tim as our Easter bunny; a Fourth of July float featuring the Utech/Hanschu families; Scarecrows in the fall; Reign Anduss playing Santa to Mikayla Antoszyk at the annual Festival of Lights; Cousins Micah Schubert and Jana Wick (Pat's daughter) entertain at family reunion, playing two old ladies gossiping; the California Sisters serving at the May Tea. In the center is Jessica Gilbert and Emily Staatz behind masks made to preserve their faces for posterity.

Don't Let it Get Monotonous

"So where would you like to go for lunch tomorrow?" asks my friend Tony—this Friday appointment has become a pattern. "Let's try something different," he says.

For Tony, who has lived two decades beyond the biblical promise of three-score and ten, lack of monotony has been a lifetime quest.

It probably started long before Tony trekked across his family's wheat field west of town as a young sprout, with his brothers in tow, to see the train for themselves. I know it continued when he decided to join the Navy and see the world. Lack of monotony was one reason he chose to settle in San Francisco when he retired, although he made regular trips to Ramona each year.

Tony's mind is always curious, and continually searching for adventure—whether he's taking a trip to the auctioneers' convention, creating the belly button fathometer (which measures body fat) or taking a trek to the latest dinosaur exhibit in Hays.

"You just can't let things get monotonous," Tony said to me as we drove toward Woodbine. "Turn east," he commanded, "we'll take a different route."

Just the directive to turn east made things interesting for me—I'm still a left-right kind of person, and north-south, east-west directives make my brain spin.

"Monotony will get you, if you aren't careful," Tony went on and then he chuckled. "Remember when I sent the checks to my niece and nephew for graduation, and I made them out for $99.99?"

I remembered. And I also knew why he'd done it.

"I could send them a $100 bill but they'd spend it tomorrow and never remember it. But $99.99 they'll remember." So instead of a twenty-dollar bill, a loved one might receive $33.33, or instead of $50 a $67.89. I, too, love the interesting, the memorable, the quixotic, and loath the mundane.

When Tony made Ramona his home base a couple of years ago, monotony was one of the things he was worried about. "In San Francisco there is something new happening every few minutes!" he said to me. He and I both knew that in Ramona you could go all day—maybe even all week—without something happening to relieve the boredom.

Monotony is something neither Tony nor I can tolerate. Quiet? Yes. Slower pace? Okay. But let's not get redundant.

Conversations can even get monotonous, with, "How are you?" and "I'm fine, thank you." Predictably, continuing on with, "So what you think of this weather we're havin'?"

Words get monotonous. My old friend, Doc, held the belief that in order for a word to be truly interesting it needed more than three syllables. None of this "whoa," "cool," "wow" stuff with expletives deleted. He loved batting words around like discombobulate and plethora.

One time just for the kicks of it, I wrote a piece of poetry filled with made-up words. I was doing it to relieve the monotony of a boring speaker:

> *Tuberlundin blockinstein, doesn't tell you what I mean, Blibberwaken clumdifew will not mean a thing to you. Gibeenfalder, migglewalk, isn't normal people talk, Whoominhollder, redunderation, discombobbled communication.*

What lengths we go to keep things interesting. It's why we plan events in Ramona, like Fourth of July parades, tea parties, scarecrows and Christmas light extravaganzas. We can't let life get ho-hum, boring, dreary, same-old-same-old, or monotonous.

"Turn west," Tony commanded as we headed for home. "I'll show you a new way to Ramona that I bet you've never taken."

It's just another day in the country, and I'm on a quest for something unusual, something interesting. When the day is over I'll watch the sun set over the prairie. Brilliant colors, unusual clouds, breathtaking—never monotonous, I guarantee it!

Stefanie Staatz Mainville, our neighbor girl, whose baby daughter we mention in this story. Time flies! Circa 1995

As Our World Turns

In a big city, life's dramas are multiplied by as many people living there, which takes on huge proportions. But the occupants of the city register very little of this real-life soap opera going on around them.

Depending on the size of your community, you can hear an ambulance every hour but you don't know the particulars of the call. Along with your morning coffee you read about disasters in the newspapers, however, you really don't know these people. They're as faceless as the actors on the television screen.

But in a little town like Ramona, we know all the main characters in our daytime serial. If an ambulance comes into town, we can trace the sound of the siren and know where it stopped. The same goes for the Sheriff's car.

All of this "knowing" is a heavy load of info to hold about your neighbor. And no matter whether today's episode of *As Our World Turns* in Ramona is joyous or sad, cause for celebration or embarrassment, we all tune in tomorrow to see how things turn out.

In a small place, we know things about one another that the world at large doesn't know, and this calls for a heart full of compassion, a lot of understanding, and a measure of forgiveness for ourselves as well as others.

If you yell too loud at your husband, someone hears it. If you burn your trash when you aren't supposed to, someone smells it. When you go to the hospital, the grocery store, or get stalled beside the road, someone sees it. When you are absent from church you are missed and someone will probably check on you to see if you're okay. This kind of knowing is both the joy and the pain of a small town.

I thought about the compassion of *knowing* this weekend, as I watched the cars cruise around town. At this very minute, there are people driving around cities in America and no one is paying any attention, but in Ramona if you see someone drive by you usually know a part about the on-going story of their life.

For instance, my aunt Naomi, who's in her 80s, was out driving her car on Saturday. She's a gutsy lady and I knew that she was practicing. She's been confined for almost four months, recovering from a major surgery, and she wanted to make sure she hadn't forgotten how to drive.

On Sunday, I saw Frances Hanschu driving down the street—driving Clinton around town. He's been ill and was home for just a day or so, and wanted to see the spots where he had spent so many hours working. He wanted to see the alfalfa field, the cattle corral on the edge of town, the land where Rick had cut and baled hay. He wanted to drive down main street where the store he once owned now houses the Ramona Café. He wanted to go past the barbershop, by the houses of family and friends and finally home again.

Later in the afternoon, another segment of our ongoing story unfolds as our newest Ramona resident came home from the hospital, brand new and cute as a button! I can remember when the baby's mother, Stefanie, was only 5 or 6 years old.

We'd come to town for a couple of weeks in the summer and Stef would run across the road to welcome us. I called her "the reporter," because as soon as we hit town she'd be over on our porch reporting the news of Ramona—all the people who'd moved in and out, all the cats that were going to have kittens, and how many puppies they had at home.

Our little "home town reporter" has grown up, and she just brought her own wee baby girl over for a first visit. As I looked at tiny baby Allison I was reminded that it does take a village to raise a child.

Stay tuned, for another day in the country.

Jakie Brunner wipes his brow on a hot Kansas day. The overalls, pocket watch on a chain and red bandanna all symbolic of his working days on the railroad. Circa 1995

Whew, It's Hot!

Part of the charm of coming to the country was the fact that we lived in a quaint little house with a porch for sitting, windows that open to the prairie breeze and that we have a real screen door that slams. We loved hearing the country sounds. When it got really hot we just endured the heat and with true pioneer spirit attempted to regulate the temperature in the house the way our Grandma used to do—opening the windows at night and closing things down in the early morning coolness, pulling the shades, even hesitating to turn on lights because bulbs generate heat.

Meanwhile we suffered through one *hot spell* after another, thinking the worst of it would soon end. The thought of closing everything in, like we do in the winter, was hard to imagine. Sitting inside of a house where it looked like no one was home, was unthinkable.

Some of my earliest memories pre-date air conditioning by quite a bit. Every summer of my childhood found us coming back to the farm for harvest and we tried to travel at night or early in the morning so that we did not have to be out on the highway in the hottest part of the day.

My dad would say, "You could fry an egg on this asphalt," and he was probably right. The heat was hard on the old car and it was hard on the occupants.

I can recall long discussions about whether it was worse to have the windows of the car closed which meant marinating in our own sweat as we stuck to the upholstery or whether we'd feel better suffering the onslaught of the blast-furnace air coming in through the windows. Those who voted for windows open usually won and we'd arrive at our destination dry, dehydrated, windblown and cranky.

"My mother used to dip her corset in well water and put it on wet before she went out to do chores," an aunt tells me, "it was what she had to do to keep cool." I silently give thanks for the demise of corsets.

"Mom would hang wet dish towels in front of the windows," an uncle chimes in, "to cool the air." I can remember my mother trying that trick and have used it on occasion myself.

"We didn't mind the hot weather, like we do now," Aunt Naomi reminds me, "When you live in an air-conditioned house, you just want to die when you go outside. Back then, it was hot no matter where you went—we were just used to it."

When my aunts and uncles were children there was not even such a thing as a garden hose to play with, "Dad had to even carry water to the garden," my aunt reminds me. "We didn't even have a place to go swimming."

I wondered why they didn't use the stock tank. By the time I came along, my grandpa would let my cousin and me use it for a swimming pool—even though our mothers considered it awfully dirty—and we'd splash and wallow in it to our heart's content. Sometimes we'd have water fights on the scraggly lawn with a tub of water and a cup for each player.

"This is all the water you get," my mother would warn. Water was always precious in Kansas.

"During threshing time my mom would go to town to get ice so that the men would have something cold to drink at noon," Aunt Naomi tells me.

To be without ice in the summer boggles the mind of a generation that has grown up with ice cubes readily available.

"We were so excited when we got an old ice box to keep food cool," Aunt Naomi says and stops to explain that someone from Tampa delivered a chunk of ice from Herington two or three times a week for the ice box, "and you had to remember to empty the water pan underneath every day or your kitchen would be flooded!"

Well, Aunt Naomi is all excited, today! She just got a brand new Kenmore and she's like a little kid with a new toy. "I just love it," she exalts, "I can get cold water or crushed ice right in the door. It's so pretty I took a picture of it," and she laughs at her own folly.

Yes, it's another day in the country and I think I'll stop by Aunt Naomi's house for a glass of tea with lots of ice.

Once summer is in full swing, this is one day's crop of cucumbers. Who will eat them all? Circa 2004

Cucumber Take-Over

It's been years since I've had such a prolific garden. The cucumbers have taken over.

When I hauled the first bushel of potential pickles up on the porch my non-organic sister said, "Oh, no, the cucumber nightmares are starting." (It's when you go to the refrigerator in search of milk and all you find are cucumbers. It's when the cheese drawer and all the crispers are full of cucumbers, there's another load of them in the sink, you've already given bags of them to all your relatives, cucs are proliferating as we speak, and no one wants any more.)

"Can we agree on a size limit?" Jessica inquires cautiously, eyeing the day's take.

It seemed to me that the cucs were playing hide and seek. If I missed them for a day or two, we could add wheels and *drive them* out of the garden, still sweet and succulent.

"My Mom makes the best pickles out of those big ones," suggested our friend Tooltime Tim, trying to be helpful. "They're good. They taste like candy." That was a long leap for my imagination but I sure hated to see those big cucumbers go to waste.

Our neighbor, Jane, heard me talking about this creative solution for my extra cucumbers. "I've got a recipe for spiced cucumber rings from my great aunt," said Jane, heading out the door before I could offer her more produce.

A few minutes later she returned and handed me a card with tiny handwriting all over both sides. The list of ingredients was long and strange—all things I didn't stock in my cupboard: lime, alum, cinnamon sticks, red hots, food coloring, vinegar.

Well, I started to peel, seed and slice cucumbers, soaking them in water to await their transformation. Little did I know how much time these veggies and I would spend together in the kitchen.

Later when Jane brought lime from the store in Lincolnville, I read just enough of the recipe to discover that these rings had to soak in a lime solution for twenty-four hours!

By the time I got the alum and the red food coloring from the Hope grocery store, some of my carefully cut rings were disintegrating.

While I was buying canning jars at Wal-Mart in Salina, my sister said, "Is there some reason that we just don't go over to the pickle aisle and buy pickled something-or-other?"

"It's the experience," I told her. "I've never done this before and I've got to try it at least once."

Well, so far in this experience I've used more red food coloring than a healthy person should ingest in their whole lifetime. I've splashed pickle juice on my tan Donna Karan pants, the new dishcloths are permanently pink, and there's a dramatic red flourish on the wallpaper by the stove. I need a lab coat!

Tonight, as I simmered syrup for two hours, attempting to figure out if the cucumber rings were supposed to be in the pan or just watching from the sidelines, I reread the fine print, and discovered that I must once again let this red dye concoction set over night. What was the deal with our grandmothers and these long, involved recipes for frill-food?

I've now spent four days and $35 on canning supplies, and we're not even close to being done!

Today I asked Jane, "Have you ever tried this recipe?"

"Nah," she said, "I've never had time."

Tomorrow the recipe card says I'm supposed to drain that lethal red juice from the soused circles yet again—without splattering—heat and pour it back over the cucumbers for another night of inebriation, repeating the whole process on Wednesday. Then, and only then, can I seal those perfect red circles into their brand new jars.

"Good grief," I mumbled to the cucs, "We've got to be in Lawrence on Wednesday—one more day of this and I would have had to hire a pickle-sitter!"

It's another day in the country, and you know what I'm doing—draining and dying cucumbers. All I can say is, "These better be *darn tasty!*"

An old fence post, still doing its job on the Fike Farm west of Ramona. Circa 2000

Plagued by Grasshoppers

They tell me that this is the time of year that tomatoes become Christians. It's because you'll find them going to church regularly every week, and hoping to be taken home for dinner by some member of the congregation.

A couple of Sundays ago, Aunt Naomi brought a little bag of tomatoes home after church. She said that her friends had come prepared with the little red vegetables all sorted out into small paper bags that you could tuck under your arm. These people were experienced tomato-givers!

We're overflowing with tomatoes at our house, too, but I haven't taken any to church—I just make the rounds of relatives.

Once a garden begins to grow, it takes over the time schedule. It's feast or famine. Two weeks ago it was feast. This week, the grasshoppers have invaded the cucumber patch and these voracious creatures ate all the leaves. This left my darling little would-be-pickles exposed, getting sunstroke from too many ultra violet rays.

Now the tomatoes are going full speed ahead. I ask around, "Anyone need tomatoes—especially these little cherry tomatoes?" Neighbors lock their screen doors, and smiling, say "No thanks." What do you do with those little things, once you've eaten your fill in the garden and have sprinkled them liberally through all your salads?

After annihilating my cucumber patch, those nasty hoppers have moved into the tomato patch, actually taking huge bites out of my succulent big-boys. I've formulated a strategy. I'll leave those little cherry tomatoes on the vine for the grasshoppers—since the cheery tomatoes are more their size, you'd think they'd like them best. The idea is for the grasshopper plague to be good citizens, take what is offered and leave the rest alone!

My father tells me that grasshoppers never were gracious neighbors in Ramona. He's full of Kansas horror stories with grasshoppers as the main villain. He remembers seeing the grasshoppers fly into Kansas like a dark cloud, descending on their already dry and thirsty fields. He tells me that those grasshoppers were so hungry in the thirties, and there were so many of them, that you could hear them chewing if you listened closely.

My mother, who also grew up in these parts, said that the grasshoppers chewed up the crops, they chewed up the gardens—hollowing out the onions so that the outer shell was all that remained in the ground—and they even chewed on the fence posts made of hedge wood. "They chewed the bark right off those posts so they were slick," she said. "I'll never forget it."

I have difficulty assimilating the hardship my family experienced before I was born. I have never been dependent on the weather for my income.

Instead, my memories of the country are idyllic—riding through the fields with my grandpa on the hay wagon, playing in the barn loft while he milked, and stirring up cakes of chicken mash and water, which baked in the hot Kansas sun and then were ceremoniously served to the cat.

Meanwhile, my parents were struggling to survive, and wondering if the egg money would feed us another week.

My father's memories of farming are littered with dust storms and drought and ravaged by grasshoppers and hail. The good times are over-shadowed by the Depression, and the difficulty of surviving. Your driving ambition was to get away, move, anywhere!

On the other hand, my recollections of the olden days are framed by the innocence of childhood, and even at sixty, I'm free to marvel at just another day in the country.

As mayor of Ramona, Pat led the Fourth of July Parade. Two longtime dreams fulfilled: (1) riding a horse again and (2) dressed like an Indian! Circa 2004

Remembering the Olden Days

I've always been fascinated with historical reenactments. In California they did it on a big scale, recreating the time of good Queen Elizabeth, with the Renaissance Faire. We loved dressing up in our peasant dresses, and pretending for a day that we had stepped back in time.

Over the years we've done our own reenactments, on a much smaller scale, right in the backyard. I made Indian tipis for my daughter and her friends—little one-person tents to cut down the quarreling. They played Indian by the hour, by the day, setting up their camp, getting dressed in all their Indian finery, dreaming up war chants and harvest dances.

Since their tipis were too small for a campfire, my ten-year-old built a rock-lined fire pit in the middle of the circle of tents, and the kids took turns snitching flour and salt, carrots and potatoes, corn, and beans from the refrigerator, to make their concoctions of bean-spice soup and roasted bread.

Of course, I kept an eye on them and their land of enchantment. It was delightful to behold, especially in the evening as the day wore on. My little Indians were quieter, their camp was in order, they had played to their hearts' content, and as the last of the smoke from the campfire drifted up, and they sat around it talking softly, I could have sworn I'd stepped back to another era.

There are times I remember from *my* childhood that I wanted my children to experience: eating supper by the light of the kerosene lamp in Grandma's kitchen, milking cows and attempting to squirt milk into the cat's mouth, driving the team of horses back to the barn, swimming in the stock tank, and making homemade cottage cheese.

Every Schubert Family Reunion we try to do something from the past. "I want the kids to know," I tell my sister as we drag the butter churn down from the shelf, and fill it with cream.

"How long does this take?" the ever-efficient Jessica wants to know.

The one time we churned butter for the family dinner it took forever. While the kids took turns churning, Aunt Gertie told them how many pounds of butter *her mother* churned as a child—butter was a precious commodity and part of the family income. "They took that butter and delivered it to bankers and doctors in Iola," said our aunt.

After an hour of story telling and churning, we were about to give up the notion that butter would ever appear in the glass jar.

"Keep going! It's almost done!" admonished Aunt Naomi as she saw us losing enthusiasm. Within seconds the mixture in the churn took form and we had butter—we'd lived a piece of history!

When folks call and ask for a tour of our mini-museum in the old bank building, we get out our costumes from the olden days, and enjoy dragging our skirts around in the dust for a few hours, remembering the era when an ankle was not to be seen and a big bustle was a thing to be desired.

When we hanker for simplicity, we dream of renovating Green Acres—the one house we own in Ramona that still needs fixing up.

"We could make it an old-fashioned house," we dream, "with a wood stove and a hand pump beside the sink, like Grandpa had in his house when we were kids. There'd be no telephone and no electricity—just kerosene lamps for light. . ." and the possibilities are on parade.

I can see us now, in the kitchen turning out warm biscuits and homemade jam for our guests—sweat pouring down our faces—as we celebrate another day in the country.

Tim takes a refreshing dip in Herington Lake and eludes the heat at the end of the day. Circa 2001

The A/C's On!

I've never lived in a house with air conditioning. In the Napa Valley, unbearably hot weather was so seldom, and our house-building budget was so small thirty years ago, that we didn't even consider putting in central air. After all, we'd come from the Midwest and we knew how to keep a house cool—you open the windows in the evening and close them during the hottest part of the day. You hope for a little breeze, and plant shade trees!

In Ramona, our house was old and didn't even have central heat, let alone central air! Furthermore, we liked the open windows, the breeze that blew through, and the sound of country life—like the screen door slamming. We didn't need air conditioning. We were tough, Kansas stock!

"This isn't bad," we said to each other as the temperature climbed. "There'll be a break in the weather." And then it just got hotter.

When we used to come for two weeks in August, we endured the heat as part of the Kansas experience. However, once we were here for the duration, we began to wonder just how much of this *roughing it* was really necessary.

We did get air-conditioning for our Bed and Breakfast—we knew other folks wouldn't tolerate the heat—but at home, in The Ramona House, peace, quiet and hot weather reigned. We didn't like the hum of the omnipresent air conditioner. We didn't like to have the doors and windows closed in summer.

And then, that first year we lived here we gave up! It was the middle of August and so hot we couldn't breath. Jessica had started sleeping under wet towels at night so we conceded that it definitely was a little warm!

"Help," we called to Tooltime Tim. "Will you help us put that old air conditioner unit in the dining room window?" He came to our rescue, we closed everything dutifully down, and basked in the semi-stale air coming through the machine. Cool at last!

Wouldn't you know it? We no more than had the A/C in the window and the weather changed. It got cooler. We opened up the house again. There was the smell of fall in the air. We didn't need that noisy contraption after all.

The next year, we thought we could beat this syndrome by just lasting a little longer through the month of August; but we didn't make it. We tried fans whirring into the night, sleeping without sheets, soaking in Herington

Lake and a positive mindset. When we had so many fans going that our house sounded like a beehive, and the wet towels came back as a coping mechanism, we installed A/C in the window once more.

And immediately the weather changed! It was almost as if the wind shifted to the north the minute that air conditioner got plugged in. That's twice! It's coincidental, but three times is a pattern, you know.

In our third year here in Kansas we didn't even wait until August. It was July 27, to be exact, and we hauled two old decrepit air conditioners out of the garage and stuck them in our bedroom windows.

"What? You're using those old things?" Aunt Anna was concerned. "I used them on the farm for ages. Those things should have been thrown away."

But, hey, they're working. With two window air conditioners thrumming away, the good news is that Jessica can't hear the cat meowing for breakfast. I lay in front of my closed windows and have to imagine bird songs in the morning, dogs barking in the middle of the night, the rattle of the garbage trucks at daybreak on Tuesday.

A/C is not all bad; but I miss those familiar sounds of another day in the country.

And I also expect a weather change! It happens every time. We're more predictable than the Doppler.

Kansas sunflowers are the loveliest flowers, even though they are considered weeds by the wary farmer.
Not to fret, this one grew in my very own garden! Circa 2004

Time for School

"The bus is coming over the tracks," today's kids call to a laggard—this means they have another minute or two to get their hair combed or grab something to eat. And then the bus turns the corner, coming up D Street, "Hurry! It's here!"

The old timers tell me things have certainly changed from the days when they started school. Yesterday's kids often walked to school down dusty country roads. Today's Ramona kids ride the bus.

Yesterday's countryside was dotted with a country school every couple of miles. Today, there's a central school in the area, since most little towns no longer have the luxury of their own community school.

Yesterday's kids had parents who rousted them out of bed early enough to milk the cows, have breakfast, and still have time to walk to school. Today's kids arrive at school and find a breakfast option waiting for them so they won't go hungry.

Yesterday's kids had one teacher who taught all eight grades, and had twenty to thirty students all in one room. It's hard for today's generation to imagine that many youngsters living every couple of miles in this part of Kansas.

My father, Laurel Ehrhardt, lived a mile west and three miles south of Ramona in 1920. When the day came for him to start at Lincoln School, his mother handed him a little tin syrup bucket with his lunch inside, his father put him on their old horse Roxy, whacked the horse on the rump, and sent the two of them down the road to school.

Dad knew where the school was, but he didn't know English. They only spoke German at home. Thus began his formal education, and he envied the horse that got to go home.

Dad's sister, Naomi, started school when she was only five years old. She doesn't remember how she got there but she does remember their wonderful teacher, Mr. Barr. He was a good teacher and on the coldest winter days he would always have a rip-roaring fire going in the stove when the kids arrived. Class wouldn't start until they were all warmed up.

Naomi also remembers the day they finally had a school bus to take them to their new school in Ramona—by this time the Lincoln School had consolidated with the Ramona District. "I remember Henry Brubaker driving the bus into our yard to pick us up—that was really exciting," she recalls.

My uncle, Hank Schubert, started school that same year. On his first day of school his father fired up the 1918 Studebaker, loaded his six oldest children in, and drove them to Fairfield School. From that day on they walked! "I just remember I had to wear knickers on that first day and I've hated short pants ever since," Uncle Hank says.

By the time Hank's younger sister, Martha (our mom), and her two younger siblings were ready for school, they had the use of the family horse. Old Tommy was blind, crippled and permanently skinny in spite of all the concoctions the kids fed him to fatten him up. Martha (the engineer, because she was the oldest of this trio) rode in front, Frieda sat behind her with the dinner pail, and Art—the youngest—brought up the rear and handled the whip.

"Quit scooting up," Martha would scold, as she was jammed against the horse's collarbone.

"I can't help it," Frieda would lament.

"And I can't help it neither," Art would chime in from the back end as they bounced along the road to higher learning.

Yesterday's kids were lucky to get a new outfit for school—usually it was hand-me-downs. I heard someone say that getting a child outfitted for school these days costs around $400.

Yesterday's kids shake their heads, "We even bought the books at a secondhand store, or maybe from a friend's child," Aunt Gertie tells me. When she taught school the only supplies a child needed was a big Red Chief tablet, some pencils and a box of crayons. "We didn't have long lists like they do today—it wasn't nearly so complicated."

It's just another day in the country for yesterday's kids, and the town is strangely quiet. Today's kids are on the corner, all spruced up, waiting for the bus.

"Don't forget to come out on the porch and wave when the bus goes by," my neighbor's child admonishes. She wants to know that the world is noticing summer is over and today's kids are back in school.

Warren "Biff" Fike reads the morning paper at his family home west of town. The Fikes have farmed this land for almost a hundred years. Circa 1998

Nicknames

After being in Ramona for awhile, I thought I was getting pretty good at knowing who was whom, and then someone suggested I get some information from Whimpy. "Who?" I asked in bewilderment.

"Oh, I'm sorry, that's Ralph who lives next door to your aunt." Getting acquainted with a whole town was complicated enough for us girls from California, without adding nicknames.

We knew Kink whose real name is Alfred, Peanuts whose real name is Clinton and now we discovered Whimpy, who, of course, we'd known as Ralph.

The list of nicknames we've heard about goes on and on, stemming from the era in which my parents grew to adulthood. There was Babe, Papers, Bigfoot, Sleepy, Biff, Corky, Katz, Stubby, Slick, Fritz, Fuzzy and even Hooee Haas. On top of Duke, Bud, Swampy, Junior, Ears and Speedy there were initial names like AG, LJ, JR, BJ, JB, and JD, to add to the confusion.

With most of these tag names there is a story attached. I was told that Slick always had his hair slicked back with pomade—hence the nickname. Katz (cat in German) saw a cat race down the center aisle in church and called out "katz" which raised quite a ruckus during a Sunday sermon and from that day forward he had a new name.

"It seems that most of the old timers have a nickname," I complained one day to my aunt Anna.

"Oh, yes," she says with a characteristic lilt to her voice and that look in her eye which says there is something a little questionable about all of this that should not be discussed. "Your uncle Vern was responsible for quite a bit of that happening."

Uncle Vern Strickler was a character in his own right. Vern bummed on the railroad during his teenage years according to the family story even though he came from an affluent family.

"He was sowing his wild oats," is the way my uncle Hank describes it. Those wild oats included marrying Hank's beautiful sister, Bertha, before she had a chance to finish high school. Vern took his responsibilities to heart, came home to help run Strickler's store and became the number one cheerleader for the kids of Ramona. When there was a basketball game and nobody was around to take the kids to the game, Vern volunteered and as he got to know those kids, he gave them nicknames.

When I questioned my dad about all the nicknames in Ramona, he said, "Ah, some of them came from boys messing around teasing each other—you know, locker room kind of stuff."

Nicknames are like a secret code, triggering a memory of something significant that only a few people know about. It is a phenomena of friendship and community life. A nickname signifies that you are known. In the country, your reputation—earned or otherwise—follows you wherever you go. There seems to be few second chances and your nickname is a daily reminder of who you've been or what you've done. It speaks to a familiarity and shared experiences that sometimes we would just as soon forget.

I've never had a nickname, except for the shortened version of my name, until the other day. "You girls want something to do?" our friend Tooltime Tim asked. "Then let's get those limbs out of the yard over there at Green Acres so the mowing will be easier." We proceeded to do just that with load after load of fallen debris and when our own yards were cleared we started on Leon's house, next door.

"Hey, Lulu," Tim called as he returned from emptying a truck load of limbs, "Are you done over there?"

"Lulu," I grinned to myself. Hot diggidy, it's just another day in the country and I've got myself a nickname!

If you are a seasoned farmer, you know these aren't Kansas-style chickens. I actually took this picture in Bali.
But chickens are chickens, right? Circa 1992

Run Chicken, Run!

There is nothing like a bowl of homemade chicken noodle soup to bring up heart-warming memories. "My favorite story," said the young lady across the table from me at the Lutheran Soup Dinner on Sunday, "is the one about the chicken in the trunk." She looked over at her father to fill in the details.

"You see, we were going to visit my grandma Hicks," Reverend Gene Hicks began. He smiled as he sat back in his chair. "My mother wanted to do something special for her in-laws so she decided to take a fresh chicken down to them for Sunday dinner. There is a difference, you know, in how chicken tastes. Fresh chicken is so much better than anything store-bought. So we put the chicken in a crate and loaded it into the trunk of our 1937 Chevy and headed for Iola."

This chicken was like a hostess gift. Today someone might bring flowers, a box of chocolates or a bottle of wine. In 1937, the hot commodity was a live chicken from the pen in the backyard.

"Mother was so concerned that the chicken would suffocate in the trunk that she made us stop every few miles to give that chicken air. She wanted to make sure her offering of fresh meat would arrive in fine shape," Gene laughed.

I could relate to delicious country-fried chicken. My grandmother's fried chicken was legendary in our family—tasty, tender, crispy, and delicious. We each had our favorite parts—I'm chagrined now in my semi-vegetarian status to recall that the liver and the heart were the little treats I grabbed first from the platter.

I rarely got in on the butchering end of the chicken dinner. The only part I knew well was the wonderful aroma wafting from the kitchen, and the sanitized chicken parts simmering in hot grease on the stove until they were golden brown and ready for the table.

My mother, on the other hand, grew up helping with the butchering. "I didn't like that part," said my mom. "I stayed away as far as I could. I couldn't stand watching the chickens fly around after their heads were chopped off."

To ensure that there was always fried chicken on the table or in the lunch pail, Grandma raised a lot of baby chicks. Grandpa built a special place for the setting hens—like little chicken condominiums—each with their own space, fresh water, feed and even an exercise runway. "It would take three weeks for the chicks to hatch," said Uncle Hank, "and we would wait expectantly. Baby chicks in April or May meant fryers by the Fourth of July."

Grandma Schubert had her own way of butchering chickens. She'd stand on their feet while one of her children held the chicken's head straight up in the air, and then she'd slice off the hen's head with a sharp knife.

"My mother used to wring the chicken's neck off," said Aunt Gertie, adding her two bits to the chicken stories. "I'd help her pluck the hens we butchered, but she never taught me how to cut them up—your Uncle Hank had to show me how to do it." She laughed at her ineptness. "Do you know that I never killed a chicken until we were married, and I tried to do it with an ax and hit my thumb—that was it!"

To this day, I've never butchered a chicken. But, I do recall the last chicken my mother ever butchered. We were living in Garden City, and I was probably in the second grade. My father was a new pastor and some parishioner wanted to be nice to the young preacher so they brought a live rooster as a gift. But alas, my mother was already contemplating vegetarianism.

That chicken lived in our backyard for months as we eyed it suspiciously. Dad didn't want to kill it. Mom didn't want to eat it. So the rooster got more feisty and fatter every day, crowing constantly, harassing the neighborhood—which surely had an ordinance against raising chickens inside city limits.

Finally, my mother had enough and she killed, dressed and fried that rooster for dinner. We all sat looking at the platter, and even though it looked good we couldn't eat it.

As I write, I'm sure that someone is frying chicken for dinner, while we are cooking up a side dish of warm memories of another day in the country.

In the midst of raking leaves, Aunt Gertie and Uncle Hank laugh as they tell stories to their niece, Jessica. Circa 1995

The Stories We Tell

A story, especially a personal experience, told and retold, holds the original event like a kernel of truth; but with the retelling, the characters become stronger, more defined, until through the years, the story is a mixture of fable and fact.

My mother tells the story of the day she got caught eating her father's prunes. There are key elements in the story that shaped her life and mine.

First of all, Mom said she'd disobeyed. The prunes were not for any of the nine Schubert siblings to sample—they were saved for A. G. Schubert, the head of the house. He ate them every morning. They were a natural remedy for his abnormal digestive system. However, in a child's eyes, those prunes were a taste-tempting treat only enjoyed at harvest time by the regular ranks.

When Mom's older sister, Anna, caught her invading the prunes in the pantry, she asked, "What's that in your mouth, Martha?" Martha lied.

"It's a piece of coal," said the preschooler. Everyone knew, especially Anna, that Martha was not telling the truth, so little Martha was soundly punished!

When I first heard my mother tell this story, the medicinal portion of the tale wasn't evident. Furthermore, explanations of laxative would have diluted the injustice, explained away the inequity, and negated the favoritism that my child's ears believed were the heart of the story.

The part of the prune story that impacted me as a young girl was that a man received special perks and treats that were denied to a child. Every time I heard the story, my childish soul simmered with the grievance.

That story became a fable in our family and helped to shape my warrior's heart as a woman. A heart that, to this day, strives for equality and demands even-handedness that is sometimes hard to come by.

There's always a veiled reason behind the stories we tell each other, and those stories shape the family system as we tell and retell them to our children. Mom probably told me the Prune Story because she wanted me to learn that liars are punished. I totally missed the point.

The stories we tell shape the next generation's perception of their ancestors, and all too quickly, the stories are all they have left.

Coming back to Ramona has filled out the picture of the grandfather I knew only once a year on vacation. Mom is reminded of other stories when she's in her home environment—stories of her father's innovations, his far-sightedness, and his wisdom.

Town folk tell me stories of A. G. Schubert's eccentricities, and uncles and aunts share tales of his deeds—how he started one of the first threshing companies and helped found the original co-op in Ramona.

Uncle Hank tells the story of taking over the family farm, and the first time he went contrary to his father's advice.

Uncle Hank and his brother-in-law, John Lorei, were going to repair the roof of the sheep shed. John and Hank wanted to use tin to repair the roof, and Grandpa wanted them to use shingles. When John, who used to be the Schubert's hired hand before he married into the family, sided with Hank in the discussion, A. G. was outvoted.

I was aghast when I heard this story; I knew that A. G. Schubert was seldom crossed. His prowess at winning card games and arguments was legendary. I waited to hear about the blow-up, the retribution, the angry words—there was none.

"So now the chick knows more than the hen," A.G. said quietly to his son. That was it! Tin covered the shed.

As I tell you this story, I am reminded to cultivate a similar grace, so that as a younger generation takes over the reins of leadership, I can follow in Grandpa's footsteps.

It's another day in the country, and I can no longer catch Uncle Hank walking to the Post Office and ask him a question. My beloved kin have been transplanted to be near their children. I had to call clear to Colorado to make sure I'd gotten this story straight. I must admit, I'm not ready for the chicks to know more than the hen!

Jim Thompson, one of our most recent "move-ins" to Ramona, dismantles the old Sader house. Circa 2004

Ruddngghhh! Ruddngghhh!

I can hear the motor on the old white truck revving up across the street. He's still at it! Jim is working on the original property that first caught his eye on the Internet, a year or so ago, when he was still living in California.

The charm of the very misleading photograph was what first caught his attention. The price tag seemed amazingly inexpensive by California standards. The land had allure. And the next thing you know the Thompson family was in Kansas.

To make a long, sad story shorter and more hopeful, Jim tried, felt defeated by the shell of a house he'd found on the property, let the property go, someone else bought it, felt the same and offered it all back to Jim, who took them up on the now-much-sweeter-deal.

This man's been around the game board once, and he's back at square #1. So, to spruce up the property and please the city, he's tearing down an old abandoned building on the corner that used to be Mr. Sader's workshop, where he repaired small appliances.

Jim has never torn down a house before. I don't believe he's ever built one either—but he figured that ingenuity must count for something, and what goes up must come down, eventually.

About a week ago, I heard an engine gearing up in the tall underbrush in the vicinity of Mr. Sader's shop.

"Ruddngghhh! Ruddngghhh!" went the motor, and suddenly Jim, riding the old white truck like a bucking bronco, came flying out of the weeds, chained to the house. There was a resounding, rather satisfying crack—but the house did not fall down—only a few boards flew.

Again and again, the truck was attached to different vital parts of the house after they'd been weakened with a chain saw. Again and again the splinters flew, but the house did not collapse.

There's an old country adage that says, "Where there's a will there's a way." And my neighbor has certainly exercised that axiom to the inth degree. He's been flying out of the bushes, sometimes with the back of the truck several feet in the air, broken his chain, dented the truck, broken a window on

the truck, lost the muffler system and had a flat tire—but he keeps on working.

"Ruddngghhh! Ruddngghhh," goes the white truck, now sporting a longer chain.

You know that in a small town like Ramona there can be more sidewalk superintendents than worker bees. However, today, it's only the children from the neighborhood sitting on the side of the road, watching from a safe distance, chanting, "Bring it down, bring it down."

While the old building sat abandoned for at least a decade, with one window broken out and everything sagging, its underpinnings were strangely, stubbornly secure. "The back side was completely full of honey bees and the exterior siding was rotten to the core, and still it stands," says Jim, whose children are excited about a place to play, a spot for tree houses and bike paths; but for the old timers in town, who remember the house when it was in pristine condition, it's the finale on an era.

"That old house has been setting over there with one eye open," says my mom who lives across the street in her brand new home. "While it was a terrible sight, I think I might miss it."

The house finally toppled and piece by piece my neighbors are burning the wood in a little bonfire as I sit on the porch and watch small-town-entertainment.

It's my birthday and while we're freezing homemade ice cream, I'm thinking how much like a house is the body we inhabit.

The years march on, and at times I wonder if someday I'll end up like that old home, with one eye open and a really flimsy exterior—all in all, rather useless. I do pray that my super-structure is as tough as Sader's old shop, and that I'll stubbornly stand until the last of my timbers are relinquished to the fire. Then, I hope there are still loved ones around to remember who used to lived in that house and what fun we had while this was our habitation—here on yet another day in the country.

The dashboard of Old Blue, one of Tooltime Tim's defunct trucks. Circa 2005

Dashboard Tool Chest

When we first came to Ramona we found part of our Grandpa Schubert's desk stored in the house we'd purchased. It was one of those built-in desks, part of a colonnade, with a cupboard for bookshelves.

"Let's use that cupboard to store our tools," said my sister. We laughed remembering stories about how Grandpa's kids learned at an early age that they weren't to tamper with any of the things on Grandpa's desk or in that bookcase. It was strictly off limits. He had his own method of organization, and he didn't want it to be disturbed. And now we were using his desk for tools?

We tried applying our own method of organization to the tools that resided in Grandpa's bookcase—and it just never seemed to work. We'd come to Ramona with only our little blue suitcase filled with essentials: hammer, saw, screwdrivers, pliers, planes. Almost immediately we started adding to our stash of equipment needed for repairing a house and keeping it going.

As our tools multiplied, so did the containers for safekeeping. We had a jillion sizes of nails left over from projects, and dozens of different kinds of screws, fasteners, hooks, and staples. What do you do with all that stuff?

Three houses and twice the number of tool storage areas later, we're still trying to find an organizational pattern that fits. "What happened to the hammer? We have three! Anyone seen the miter box?" I ask. "It must be at the *other* house," is the usual answer.

Where are the Phillips screwdrivers? All I can find are flat tips. Where could all of these tools go?

Eventually, every well-meaning toolbox is emptied, and we end up going to the old country tried-and-true to find what we need——the dashboard of Tooltime Tim's truck.

It looks a mess, but it never fails. When we need anything, there's always something that will work on that dashboard.

That's it! I don't need a tool shed (which I have), organized like my father's, with painted outlines around all the major tools. I don't need another one of those fancy red metal tool chests (which I have) or some gizmo that is

a tool box and a step stool combined (we have two of those). I just need a dashboard!

Yesterday, out of curiosity, I inventoried all the things in a typical Dashboard Tool Chest. Here's what I found: regular pliers, screwdriver, long shank drill, 5/8" crescent wrench, tape measure, wire cutter, needle nose pliers, 3 empty chewing tobacco cans (great for storage, I've discovered) voltage meter, a ten-tools-in-one gadget still in a case (an award from work), a small empty gift box, a cow tag, some receipts, two cans of wood putty (different colors), a rubber band, masking tape, two thumb tacks, heavy duty staples, paper tablet, long drill bit extender, long Phillips bit, a pipe nipple, pocket knife, utility knife, part of a doorknob, safety sunglasses, ten AA batteries, pencil, pack of nails for air gun, ll/16" wrench, a ratchet, meter gauge, wrench, keys, ballpoint pen, putty knife, two wood drill bits, 3/8" wrench, Tampa Bank ice scraper, calculator, small light bulb, 5/6" wrench, vice grip, a part for a weed eater, door handle for the truck window (handy in case you need fresh air on that side), more keys, 4" screw with three washers attached, two dowel strips, a rag, and some sand paper.

Tooltime Tim had almost every vital tool there, except for a hammer, drill and a saw. (The drill was behind the seat, the hammer was on the floor and the Sawz-All is usually in the back of the truck.)

So here is what I've learned after spending another day in the country. You can drool over the lovely wood tool chests, the indestructible plastic carriers, the bright red designer units, and you can collect coffee cans, peg board containers and baby food jars until you are blue in the face—but if you really want to get the job done, you just keep those tools handy!

Throw 'um on the dashboard where you can actually find them.

There's a joke in Ramona that says there are more dogs than people in town. In the spring, it's probably true. Here's Emily Staatz, holding two of the puppies at her house the year we took the Dog Census. Circa 2000

Dog Dramas

Dogs have always been a drama in Ramona, namely because there are so many of them.

"They wanted me to run for mayor one time," said my 90-year-old uncle. "I told them I wouldn't touch that job with a ten-foot pole! It was because of them dogs." His voice was rising with amazing conviction. "There's way too many. Nobody wants to make any rules and if they do make 'um then nobody wants to make 'um stick!"

Ironically, when I became Ramona's mayor in 2003, I found his statement to still hold true.

Right after the weather, dogs are an important topic of conversation in a small town. We talk about whose dog is running around and whose dog is getting into the trash. We discuss whose dog is barking all night and whose dog got run over.

The dog population of Ramona proved to be so interesting that in 2000 we took an official dog census and wrote a book, *Emmy Takes a Census*. My neighbor's child and I went door-to-door discovering the name and pedigree of almost every dog in Ramona.

This morning, as I chased dogs out of my yard, I was remembering the year we came back to Ramona for the first time to actually live for a couple of weeks in the house we'd just renovated. That year, our neighbor's dog had ten puppies and Emmy announced the new arrivals the minute we hit town. Within days the proud mother dog was parading her pups around and before we could count them, all ten had discovered our yard. From that moment on, nothing was safe.

If you stepped out of your muddy shoes to go into the kitchen for a drink of water, at least one shoe was gone when you exited five minutes later. If you put down the pruning shears while you stooped to pick up clippings for the compost pile, those shears were gone before you got the kink out of your back. Nothing was exempt.

We lost sunglasses, drinking glasses, screwdrivers and even a hammer.

We lost nippers, gloves, socks and finally shirts off the clothesline. Ten puppies were the complete recipe for mischief, and I must admit, a lot of fun to watch.

The final straw came the day we were getting ready to return home to California. In the hub-bub of saying goodbye and getting the car loaded, one small overnight bag was left on the sidewalk. As we turned the corner toward the highway, catching a last fleeting glimpse in the rear-view mirror of our lovely little country cottage with the white picket fence, I slammed on the brakes.

"Those dumb dogs have one of our suitcases," I bellowed as I made a fast U-turn back toward the house. My sister was yelling out the window, "No! Bad dogs! Drop that underwear!" as I skidded to a stop. Only minutes had elapsed, but our stuff was everywhere.

Ten little dogs had fought over the bag. In the tumble, the lid came open. Now there was more than enough loot for everyone. Crunchy toothbrushes were snapped in two, lotion was gnawed on, the shampoo was promptly bitten into and at least one puppy was foaming at the mouth. For that matter, so was I!

The whole neighborhood was laughing as they hunted through the grass for hair brushes, face powder, lipstick and face creams. There were teeth marks on everything, including the suitcase—a year-long reminder of what mayhem puppies can create.

The next year, when we arrived in town to spend another day in the country, Emmy came running to announce that two of their cats had kittens. "Hallelujah," my sister exclaimed, "It's only cats!"

Erich and Tony survey the land and Tony's cattle—this was the Alpha herd. Circa 1996

Seedless Watermelon

One year Betty tried growing seedless watermelon in her garden. What a conundrum. We find it difficult to imagine a growing thing without seed for the next generation. It reminds me of some of our bachelor farmers in town.

"I told Erich that he and I are like two old telephone poles with the lines down," says Tony ruefully, "Nothing going on from here."

I listen to these two old friends talk about their fences, their fields, their new calves, and I smile. Both of them grew up right outside of Ramona. Now they live in town.

"All it took was that winter of 1983," Erich says, "that one was a doozy with snow higher'n my pickup truck on the roads. I was snowbound out there on the farm for seven days. You try that sometime. I moved to town!"

Well past three-score-and-ten, these two are such a good thing to have in Ramona. They are always supportive, attending, doing their part. It's a shame they have no progeny, because they have such good hearts—sweet and unspoiled, giving back to the earth into which they will eventually return like their forefathers before them, back into the soil that gave them sustenance.

Tony and Erich care passionately about the land. Erich says, "You won't find a weed in my fields—they're clean." And he's right; there aren't even sunflowers blooming in his ditches.

Tony meanwhile chops bull thistles in his pasture to keep his ground weed-free, and himself occupied. They both are concerned that farmers are letting the pastures grow up in junk trees.

"Look at that field," says Tony as we drive to Herington. "Next year it will take another twenty-five percent *more* effort to clean it up than it would have taken this year. And every year you wait, you can add another twenty-five percent." Who will care so passionately after they are gone?

I remember when I used to see Jakie's car go by on his way to the Post Office. A little shriveled chili-pepper of a man, he was still spicy at eighty-eight. As I'd batten down the hatches at the Ramona House for the winter to head for California, I always wondered if Jakie would survive the coming season. At his age, he was sure he wouldn't, and he'd give us instructions about the flowers and what to do in his absence. And then one spring he was

gone, and now we own his house, plant gardens in his yard, and tell stories about him.

Tony waves to me as I water the flowers, "I'm going out to spray weeds," he calls. "Have a nice day."

It used to be this was the time of year when he'd say, "I'm going out to *train my cattle*," which meant he'd entice them toward the holding pens with hay and grain cubes so that they would come willingly the day they were going to market. Now someone else raises the cattle for him, and his pasture is rented—life's seasons have changed.

It's the end of August and while my California instincts tell me that there is still time to plant a "winter garden," I hesitate. The seasoned gardeners in town are just letting things be.

Kink is waiting for his sweet potatoes to mature, Betty's cleaned up all her corn stalks and thrown them on her burn pile, and David mowed over the cucumber patch. They are harvesting, canning, clearing away, stacking, cleaning up—they aren't planting. I'd better follow their example.

Meanwhile my garden at Jake's Place, where it grows in partial shade, is flourishing. I have some wonderful Burpless cucumbers, a second crop of string beans, and of course tomatoes to pick.

It's another day in the country, and I will quarter and divide these fruits of the soil for my sustenance, savoring each bite and marveling at their home-grown flavor—just as I shelter and savor the old souls who live in this small town.

Potatoes from Pat's garden. There's absolutely nothing more satisfying than digging potatoes in the fall—except, maybe eating them! Circa 2002

Do Mashed Potatoes Go With That?

When it comes to food, we're pretty experimental. Exotic dishes and gourmet meals have become a staple at our table. And we don't even think about it. Basimati rice and Indian curry, one night, homemade tamales or enchiladas another. Stir-fry vegetables and Chinese noodles are another favorite. And then our mother came to town.

"Come eat with us tonight," we offered.

"What are you having?" she wanted to know.

"Majedra," I said. (I don't know how you really spell this—it's just how it is pronounced. And I don't know what culture it hails from—it's just delicious.)

"What's that?" she said, wrinkling her brow and looking slightly stunned.

"It's lentils served over rice with lettuce, lemon, fresh onions and garlic salt for seasoning. If we have feta cheese we'll crumble some of it over the top. It's sooo good!"

Well, she wasn't convinced but she was game to try. As she tentatively tasted this new food grouping she said, "Where do you girls get these ideas? I never cooked anything like this."

"Haven't you ever tried new recipes from some magazine?" We asked. "Don't you buy recipe books with lovely pictures and cook new dishes just for fun?"

The answer was "NO!" and she chuckled. "I guess I just always cooked what my mother cooked, and then when I got married I learned to make some new dishes from Laurel's side of the family—that's it."

"I never ate rice until you guys came," says Tooltime Tim, who is brave enough to eat with us. Tim's a meat-and-potatoes-kind-of-guy, and not at all impressed by the need to sample a wide variety of food groups.

I asked him what was the most unusual food he'd tried. "I guess I'd have to say Chinese," he said. "That egg-foo-yung stuff—I might have tasted it before, but I never knew what it was made out of." To Tim's credit, he not only tasted egg foo yung but he learned to make it!

Tim's a little like Mikie on the old breakfast food commercials on television—we watch Tim's reaction to food and then say with glee, "He *likes* it!

Times certainly have changed! The world has gotten smaller and more exotic. Bookstore shelves are filled with interesting recipes from around the world. You can taste test cuisine from almost any culture you can name—in the city that is! Here in the country, exotic is probably Chinese food, and a cultural adventure is going to the Mexican café in Lost Springs.

We laugh at the memory of Dad on his first excursion to Taco Bell, which just happened to be his granddaughter's favorite place to eat. "Just order me one of those beanie things," he suggested to Jana.

"Grandpa," she countered, "They've almost *all* got beans in them."

While it's fun to try new dishes, the foods we are familiar with are still dear to our hearts. We've learned to love the kinds of things our grandmother made. We love butterballs in homemade chicken noodle soup, and yet there was a time when butterballs were a strangely foreign idea.

Uncle Hank was a little boy sitting at a neighbor's table, with his older brother Albert, when he first spied *buterglase*. He only knew enough about them to know he didn't like them, and he also didn't want to offend the hostess, so he sneaked them off his plate and into his pocket, where his sisters finally found them, and afterwards had to scrub like mad to get the grease out of his britches.

I can remember when the country treat was something called *schnit soup* made with dried fruit and often served cold. It made me gag! I hated it! Who would believe I'd grow up to be such a food explorer?

It's another day in the country and our cousin Janet brought fajitas for dinner on the Fourth of July while Jessica made her famous chili relleno dish.

Mom was invited and she said warily, "What are you having?"

Jess explained and added, "You could bring something so that you'd be sure there was a dish you liked."

There was a moment of silence on the other end of the phone, and Mom said, "Would mashed potatoes go with that?"

The Ramona House in the fall. Isn't it beautiful? We love this little house and think she looks like a fine lady wearing a bonnet. Circa 2000

For Everything There's a Season

It was the Solstice this week—that magical date on the calendar that declares a shift of seasons. There is a certain feeling in the air as nature gently reminds us that it is time to wind down, gather in the fruits of our harvest to sustain us, put up the storm windows, and stack the wood in preparation for winter.

There's crispness in the air, come fall, and a glorious color, as the leaves change from green to gold. Communities call celebrations and revel in the fact that a summer season has been good, and now fall signals the time for rest—whether that is the people resting or the ground laying fallow.

Born on a farm, raised on a farm, beginning his own family on a farm right here near Ramona, my father made a huge life decision when he was still in the spring of his life—to go away to college. He left the farm, and this decision shaped the rest of his days.

In the fall of Dad's life when he got close to retirement, though, the country called out to him, and he created what we called a mini-farm, in Oregon. He had space, and he could raise some calves, and a few chickens. Mom and Dad could have a big garden, and smooth and green pastures, with white fences enclosing their boundaries. "This is it!" said my dad.

"I don't ever want to move again," said my mother who had survived way too many moves during her years as a minister's wife. Thirty years passed, and time took its toll—my folks needed to leave the farm, because the winter of their life had come.

I stood in the haymow of Dad's barn a couple of weeks ago, looking out across the farm, remembering all the times our ancestors moved "off the farm." It happened in the 1930s, the 1940s, the 1950s, the 1960s, and here again in the 2000s. What is this ancient tug that draws us back to country living?

I was five years old when we first moved off the farm outside of Ramona. When I was nine, my grandpa Schubert moved off his farm and into town. When I was thirteen Grandpa and Grandma Ehrhardt moved off their farm. They went to Lincoln, Nebraska, a college town, where several years later I went to school, and had the privilege of eating dinner at their table after church each week. While Grandma and I prepared the meal, Grandpa sat in the living room and talked to himself—that was always a phenomenon that intrigued me. He was still processing this shift in lifestyle.

"What's a man supposed to do in the city?" he'd say to himself. "There's nothing here."

Grandma would hear his mutterings and say, "Listen to him going on like that. I'd die before I ever went back." And here I stood in the middle of their dilemma remembering how it broke my heart when they left the farm.

For me, the farm stood for all things good—fresh roasting ears from the garden, crispy fried chicken, cousins to play with, feather beds, and mysterious attics. The farm meant wide-open spaces, riding horseback, the smell of fresh-cut hay, the sound and smell of cows being milked in the early morning hours, the creak of the windmill, and the cold tank water for splashing in on hot summer days. For Grandma, on the other hand, the memories were a harsh and impoverished reality.

When I was eighteen, Uncle Hank moved off the Schubert family farm northwest of Ramona, and it was sold. It took our family awhile to adjust to the fact that the "home place" was no longer home.

"I was ready to leave," my uncle says. "We'd had several years when it was so hot and dry. Why, I remember Gertie and I, in that old Kaiser car, driving around handing out Sale Bills. The sun was so hot that you couldn't hold your hand on the dashboard—118°. I didn't know what I'd do, but I was ready to quit farming."

And the seasons change—another leave-taking from the farm is called for, with the Sale Bill already posted for Mom and Dad's Oregon farm. We're not quite sure what we're going to do either, but we're trusting that for everything there is a season, and a proper time for everything under heaven.

In the midst of change, there will be yet, another day in the country. Ramona isn't the farm, but it's close!

Schubert relatives marvel that their hands have become their mother's hands. Circa 2003

I'm Becoming You

There was never a "home place," in the scheme of my growing-up years. Throughout my life I've lived in at least twenty-five houses. Our family was always on the move, although my beginnings were right here outside of Ramona on the very land that my grandparents had farmed.

When my parents first married, they lived in the house where Dad grew up. You know, I forgot to ask him what that felt like. I wonder now, did he feel trapped in the same dull routine of farm life in the 1930s?

When I asked my mother about this, she said they were more hopeful than anything. "We were planning for the future and scheming ways to increase our livestock and better our lives," she said.

As it is so often the country thing to do, Uncle Hank lived in the same house as his parents. "So what was that like?" I asked.

"I felt right at home," he said with a twinkle in his eye. And then he laughed, "I did find myself doing all the things that my parents used to have to do."

That was a strange feeling—a reminder that you're the one in charge, all grown up now. "I did some things a little different," my uncle admitted, "because Dad had always told me that the place was mine now, the crops were my responsibility and I was supposed to do them my way. So I did!"

Last night we were rummaging around in the attic of the Buxman home where our buddy, Tooltime Tim has lived since he was two years old. We were looking for some of his old toys for our museum display in Ramona.

"So what does it feel like to be living in the house where you grew up?" I wanted to know.

He looked at me with a quizzical expression. "Feel like?" he asked frowning. "I don't ever think about it. It just IS."

Well, there's the difference between me and most folks. I'm always thinking about stuff like that—it's the bane or the gift (whichever way you look at it) of being a writer.

The other day, my daughter called from California. "How is the country mouse?" she asked.

I assured her that the country mouse was quite content and then recited the Ramona news in a nutshell—the rain (of course, we have to talk about the weather), the graduation celebrations, the art show for the kiddies, and the latest fixer-up projects.

"It's 90° in California and I'm catching the last afternoon rays of sun on the back porch," said Jana in an eat-your-heart-out style, "While it's chilly in Kansas, I'm running around in my bikini, watering plants." She paused.

"Sometimes, I feel like I'm becoming you, Mom," Jana said with a catch in her voice. "I'm doing all the things that I remember you doing. I'm living in your house, sleeping in your bedroom, tending your flowers and I'm the age that you were when we moved into this house."

She's right! There is a way that we become our parents, year by year. I remember that feeling. I recall the day I looked down at my hands and saw my mother's hands. It was quite a shock. "These aren't my hands at all," I thought to myself, "they're Mom's!"

And here I am back in Ramona. While I'm not living in the house of my ancestors, I am walking the same ground as those generations before me. I'm tending the flowers, mowing the lawn, creating pretty little things, just like my mother, grandmother and great-grandmother did. Sometimes, as I spend another day in the country, I think of them and say, "I'm becoming you!"

Here's Em, our precious neighbor child who constantly enriches and transforms our time in the country. Circa 1998

Does This Mean You're Staying?

When my sister and I moved to Kansas in the year 2000 we were traveling light. First of all, we didn't know just how long we'd be here. Could we survive? Could we make some kind of living? Would we really like it full time? Or would we yearn for city life and California's mild, consistent climate—among other things.

The second reason for traveling light was the age-old question, "Where do you put this?" The Ramona House is small and doesn't even have closets. So, we brought what we called "Our Country Clothes," and left all the city things behind.

Every once in a while we'd say, "I wish I had *that* in Ramona," referring to whatever we remembered having packed away in California storage.

"One of these days we'll just go get your stuff," our buddy Tooltime Tim would say, "you just wait and see."

Well, this was the summer for retrieval. We hitched Tim's trailer behind his truck and headed for California. Along the way we joked as to how we would look once that trailer was full of our accumulated possessions. "Like the Beverly Hillbillies in reverse," we decided. (Being the oldest, I was nominated to sit up on top of the load in the wicker rocker.)

For anyone who has lived in one spot for thirty years you know that going through your stuff is a tedious, and sometimes painful experience. Once Jessica's boxes were loaded, we started on the garage, which housed my family's history.

Tim surveyed the mountain of things emerging and said, "Just tell me what is going and I'll start loading it on. Are we taking the tipi poles?"

The tipi poles went on first—down the middle of the trailer. These poles were nonsense to anyone else looking on, but symbolic for me. Where would I get twenty-five foot lodge pole pine to put up my tipi in Kansas? I'm sure there's an answer to that question from a whole bunch of people with prairie ingenuity, but I didn't know what it would be, so the poles came with us.

Just how do you categorize, prioritize, sort, discard, file away, classify, arrange, group, sell, and throw away part of your life? At a garage sale these things wouldn't be all that valuable. To me, however, they were infinitely useful.

When we were finished sorting we had several tons of miscellaneous goods loaded on that trailer, braced, boarded, tarped and strapped into place. It's an interesting sensation to pull your life along behind you. It definitely slows down your accent and descent on curvy mountain roads.

At fifty-five miles per hour we had plenty of time to contemplate our choices and think about the future. "Where *were* we going to put all these things in Ramona?"

"These things won't be moved again," I told Tim. "We're either using them up or getting rid of them. No more cross-country travel for this load of stuff."

So, did this mean we had honestly, truly, really, *moved* to the country?

For all of my little neighbor Emily's life, I've been her transient friend, her part-time neighbor, her pseudo-grandmother, and her summer-time guardian angel. Each time we left Ramona and headed for California she would begin questioning as to just when we would return.

"Would it be before Christmas?" she'd want to know. "Will you return in time for my birthday?"

And then we came for a whole summer, a whole year, two years and she still isn't sure that she can trust our presence.

"How long will you be here?" she'd ask.

We'd give her a hug and say, "For awhile."

On the day we drove into town with the trailer loaded she ran out to welcome us home. "Does this mean your staying?" She wanted to know.

Well, it's another day in the country, and "Yep, Em, we're staying."

Jessica and Jim Brunner delivering The Ramona News, our town newsletter (with over 300 out-of-town subscribers) that keeps everyone reading from the same page. Circa 2001

Driving Around Town

"I just drove around town last night," said Aunt Naomi, "for something to do." There are times when she just needs to see a friendly face—talk to someone for a change of pace. "I'd already visited with my legislator (translation: heard the local political news on TV) and talked to the cream puffs (she'd been baking). I just sit on my porch and nothing different ever happens, so I decided I'd drive around town and see what's happening somewhere else."

Well, Ramona is a very small town—five blocks east and west, five blocks north and south, A-F and one through five. It doesn't take long to cover the territory.

"So what did you discover?" I asked.

"That's the trouble, I didn't see a single thing different," she said with a fretful look on her face. "Nothing *ever* happens when I drive by. There wasn't even a soul outside."

We went on talking about the people who used to drive around Ramona, just like she does. Uncle John used to drive around town. He was a man of action, loved helping people, and couldn't stand to be sitting still for long.

I remember the day of the Ramona Centennial in 1987. My cousin and I blew in from California with our cameras, ready for the celebration. We were out early in the morning planning our shots of the parade route, and there was our uncle, John Lorei, already parked on main street. He was anxious to see who else would be driving around town that day.

"Your uncle Kenneth used to drive around like that," Aunt Naomi continues—now he's gone.

"Leon would always drive around," I interjected. "Remember how he'd smile and wave, and sometimes stop and chat?"

It's not just oldsters who drive around town, teenagers do it, too. No matter what our age, none of us want to miss excitement—if it's happening. Jayme used to drive around town with his stereo speakers booming in the trunk of the car. We could *feel* him coming, the vibrations were so strong, long before his car appeared. Now he's a family man with too many things to do other than cruise the streets of Ramona.

Whimpy's been retired a long time, so he drives around now and waves on his way to the Post Office. Kink drives by, taking the long way from his house to main street—probably to warm up his truck.

"And here I've started it," Naomi confesses. "Driving around to see what's going on."

There's something comforting about seeing the inhabitants of our small town drive by. Every time I see Kink driving slowly in his gray and white pickup, it's like seeing a knight on his white horse circling the town, and like sentinels of old, signaling that "All is well."

I like seeing Jim cruise the streets in his golf cart. Sometimes he gives me a ride. "Is this the 9:30 bus?" I'll ask.

"Sure," he says, "come on, let's go check out the city streets." And we drive around town.

I like living in such a small puddle that one can't help being known! I like knowing the sound of Tooltime Tim's truck driving across the railroad tracks heading into town—I'd recognize it blindfolded. I used to love hearing Uncle Hank's pick-up drive by early in the morning on his way to work. Now, he and the pick-up are both retired.

"Honk, when you drive by," we told him. "We need an alarm clock."

So, he'd tap the horn at our house, even though it was still dark outside, and he knew we were snuggled down under the covers.

"It's another day in the country," the horn was saying, "and I know you're in there." That little sweet connection just made our day!

Cole Svoboda was nine years old when this picture was taken of him helping his father, A.J., bale hay on his Uncle Tim's farm. Circa 2002

You Can Drive!

City kids learn about buses, trolley cars, and fast transit trains. Kids in the country learn to ride horses, drive cars, trucks and tractors when they are barely tall enough to see over the steering wheel. I wanted so badly to be a country kid when I was growing up.

One of my first memories of being at the controls of anything moving was a hot summer afternoon outside of Ramona, when my grandfather was heading back from the field after a long day of stacking hay. He turned to me, his tag-a-long, handed me the horses' lines, and said, "Here, hold these—you can drive the hay wagon back to the barn."

Truth was, Grandpa's horses, old Jim and his teammate, could have taken that wagon back to the barn on their own recognizance, but I was thrilled to be holding the lines. I'd never before felt so powerful.

Like my father before me, tractors have always held a fascination, and perhaps if I'd grown up on that farm west of Ramona, I would have learned to drive Dad's tractor at the age of eight or nine, like my young friend Cole, who proudly powered his dad's tractor around the field, while his father rode the baler.

My Dad grew up driving a team of horses around and around the fields, working the ground, from early childhood on, and his memories of those chores are not always pleasant. So, it probably never entered his mind that his daughter would hanker for that kind of opportunity. But I yearned to be able to drive—horses, tractors, cars and trucks.

Our family stories are studded with tales of driving forays. Aunt Naomi would beg her older brother, Laurel (when he was in high school) to let her drive the Model A, and he'd agree so long as they drove out past the Schubert farm (where his girl friend lived), and Naomi would promise not to tell their mother where they'd been.

My mom, in turn, begged her older brother, Hank, to let her drive the family car home from school. He was hesitant because he remembered some of her early forays in that car—like the time she drove around and around the house and forgot which pedal to push to stop the car, and finally drove straight into the lilac bush in the front yard to end forward progress.

My little friend Emily, who lives across the street from us in Ramona, wants so badly to be tall enough to drive my car. Ever since she was tiny, I would bend the rules and let her sit on my lap, and steer as we drove the deserted streets of town.

When Em got too big to sit on my lap, she began her campaign, "When will you let me drive your car?" She's made all kinds of promises regarding this endeavor, including reminding me that some day I will be so old that I'll need a chauffeur! She keeps measuring her legs, adding high-heeled boots and saying, "Am I tall enough yet to reach the pedals?"

My first adventure with driving a tractor came in unexpected fashion just recently. No one was available to drive Tooltime Tim's tractor, and hoist the bucket up in the air so Tim could stand in it and decorate the huge cedar tree in his front yard for Christmas. In my heart I was just aching to do the job, and I can't even remember if I volunteered or he just said, "Will you help me?"

"Would I? Oh, my, YES!" I thought he'd never ask!

Patiently, he explained the controls and I climbed into the lop-sided seat. One part of me felt like I was ten years old—thrilled, exhilarated at this great honor, and proud to be asked to perform the task. I knew just how Cole felt last summer.

"You have to stay close to the tree," Tim instructed. "Dodge those stumps. Can you do it?"

Well, Saturday, the weather warmed again briefly and Tim said, "You ready to help me take those lights back down?" I was Johnny-on-the-spot, climbed up on that old tractor, braced myself on that rickety seat, and put the tractor into low gear. There's something so exhilarating about being trusted to do this job, which may seem rather simple and mundane to you.

Oh, the thrill of spending another day in the country—once again I had the chance to drive!

David Staatz helps Tim Steinborn make sausage using the old family recipe handed down from one generation to another while Emily watches. Circa 2002

Butcher's Blend

Right about this time of year we always butchered," says my Uncle Hank. "It was after the holidays when your grandmother was ready for a whole week's worth of hard work!"

Butchering days were exciting—like a huge family reunion with grandparents, married sisters, uncles, aunts and cousins coming to help with the ritual as well as share in the bounty.

My uncle went on to explain the list of chores, which would supply the family meat for the year. "On the first day they'd kill the hogs, scald and clean them, and then hang them in the back bedroom to cool." That tells you how cold the bedrooms were—like a walk-in refrigerator.

"The next day my grandpa would render the lard—twenty-five to thirty gallons of it or more," my uncle continues, and as he tells the story, I imagine the big iron kettles filled with fat, the hot fire, the straining, the skimming, the pouring, the pressing and the finished product turning satin-smooth, snow-white, and hard in the storage crocks.

As the work unfolds, I realize these thrifty ancestors of mine used everything but the squeal! Day three was for sausage making—blood sausage, head sausage (cheese), regular sausage and liver sausage. "They took the brains out and Mom would fry it for breakfast—kinda like scrambled eggs," Uncle Hank tells me. "They pickled the tongue and sometimes the feet." (By this time I'm getting a clue as to why my mother wanted to raise my sister and me as vegetarians.)

"My dad had the recipe for sausage," says Hank, "it was mostly just how much pepper and salt to add—we never put in garlic like some folks did." He begins to smile. "I remember when I was in high school and some of the kids would open up their dinner pail and the garlic was so strong a blue flame would come out."

Day four was for salting down the hams, shoulders, and bacon for putting in the smokehouse.

"When you're done with all the work of butchering and sausage making, you have a pretty good idea of what's in that meat," says my friend Tooltime Tim. "You know it isn't just Butcher's Blend."

But in our family there are stories about unwanted *mystery* ingredients in sausage. Like the time Grandpa Ehrhardt cut his finger when he was butchering. Grandma came to his rescue with a new-fangled Band-aid.

Later in the day, Grandpa was hunkered down over the washtub mixing sausage when he realized the Band-aid was missing. It was a family emergency. Every available hand was called into action as nimble fingers sorted through the ground beef and seasoning in search of the illusive bandage. After what seemed like hours, fingers chilled to the bone, they gave up. Grandma was sober, and chagrined.

Every year, relatives in California waited to smell her sausage coming in the mail. Every year, they "oohed and ahhhed" over the delicious country flavor. She couldn't disappoint them. "With my luck," Grandma said, envisioning the most opinionated of the aunts, "I'm sure Aunt Lizzie will get the one with the Band-aid."

Since grinding meat was hard, Grandpa got smart and hooked up the grinder to the wheel of the car—they had automation. But Uncle Kenneth refused to use anything but his hand for stuffing in the meat and one time he lost the tip of his middle finger to the cause. That year Grandma threw out half-a-tub of meat.

Only once did I get in on the butchering ritual before we moved away from Ramona. It was at my grandpa Ehrhardt's farm and he'd raised the steer. While I loved Grandma's sausage and Grandpa's home-cured dried beef, I didn't particularly like thinking about the fact that this meat had been walking around earlier and even had a name.

It's another day in the country and there are no more chicken massacres in our family and no week-long butchering sessions. I must admit that meat is much easier for me to eat, if we haven't been intimately acquainted.

Snow geese landed in a field outside of town. You could hear them calling to each other, from the ground, in the air, circling the area in search of food. Circa 2003

If I Could Do It All Again

"People say they wouldn't change a thing, but I would," the song plays on my radio. "If I had my life to live over again, I'd of done a lot of things different."

When the comedic writer, Erma Bombeck, lost her fight with cancer, she sat down and wrote a list of things that she would do differently if she had her life to live over.

The first thing on her list was about going to bed when she was sick, instead of pretending the earth would stop turning if she wasn't at her desk. She goes on to mention a pink candle sculpted like a rose, and how she would have used it before it melted in storage. She mentions friends she wished she'd invited for dinner, and the rambling relative that she regrets not listening to.

I read through the list and thankfully, joyfully, jubilantly realized—especially since I have come to live in the country—I was doing all the things on her list and more!

We used to play this little game on our birthdays. One of us at the table would ask, "If you had six months to live, what would you do?"

Top on my list was always, "Go to Ramona and fix up that little house on the main street!"

Several houses later, and now living in Ramona, I still ask myself that question quite regularly. And the answer varies, depending upon the time of year.

One day in December it was, "I'd go to Branson, Missouri. That's what I'd do in a heartbeat!" So we went!

Another time I said, "I'd write stories and call them "It's Another Day in the Country." And I have!

Now I answer, "I'd publish those stories in a book." And here it is!

When my kids were little I vowed, "I'll play with my children and listen to them carefully." So I did. It became a habit, and I still love listening to the kids in town. They report to me what they are doing and when their new puppies and kittens arrive, and ask for help with school projects. I love it.

My list goes on: "I'll take a chance and tell you how I feel." So I do. "I'll talk to that stranger, listen to your story, paint that picture, lose weight, buy those boots, plant those exotic flowers that may not survive in Kansas, forgive everything—even whoever stole my camera."

This stance has become a way of life—this living in the moment. Truly living! Not just going through the motions.

C'mon, make yourself a list. Take the risk of living in the moment! You know the greatest risk in life is not risking at all! People may think you're a little crazy. They'll wonder what weird idea you'll come up with next. But it's worth the risk, believe me!

And it all starts with the decision to cherish the relationships we have with those we love, even if they're a pain-in-the-neck sometimes. And it continues on as we seize every moment and relish it, whether it's painting ceilings or fertilizing the flowers that are springing up in the yard.

I've vowed to live every moment fully, to hug life wholeheartedly, to risk being close, to feel pain and pleasure and be grateful for every nuance.

What would I change? I'd have accepted this modus operandi when I was thirty. It's another day in the country, and I'm so grateful that on most days I still feel that age, anyway.

Frost on the trees turns Ramona into a fairytale kingdom. Circa 2003

Winter Chill

When the first winter chill became noticeable, we put on our California winter clothes and shivered.

The locals said, "You cold? This ain't cold, *yet*."

And then when the wind started blowing and snow flurries were in the air, and we had added all of our layers upon layers of clothes, Ramona residents said, "This is nothin'. Just you wait until it gets *really* cold."

"Code is code," we muttered in our mittens.

This was the kind of cold that seeps under the doors, across a room, into your feet, your bones, your fingers, and leaves you fidgety, and dreaming of warm sunny porches on a summer afternoon, savoring a good book. In this weather, you don't dare dream iced tea or beaches with foamy surf—it's just too cold to contemplate.

The locals are full of wisdom as to how we can survive.

"You need one of those rag snakes to put in front of your door," Aunt Gertie suggested.

"To stop the draft through *this* house," I countered, "one of those three-foot critters won't do. I need me a tropical-sized python!"

"You need to get some plastic from the lumberyard and put it over your windows," said our trusty handyman. "Once you tape it in place you can heat it with a hair dryer and stretch that stuff out, and never know it's there—it'll help."

Plastic on my windows? You've got to be kidding. It looked tacky! But about the second week of the cold whipping around my legs as we sat down to supper, I headed for the lumberyard, and got several of those kits for windows. Pride would not stand in my way.

I'd always wondered what the deal was with people nailing roofing material around the bottom of their houses. It looked awful! We tore all of ours off the Ramona House several years ago; but then we weren't here in winter, and we didn't know the benefits we'd lost. Last month, I had to go buy more of that stuff, and we tacked it all back up in an attempt to keep the pipes from freezing.

About the fourth time the water pipes were frozen and Tooltime Tim crawled under our house with his blowtorch, I said, "Isn't there a way to prevent frozen pipes?"—other than fix our foundation, which we couldn't do in cold weather.

"Ah, you just never know," he answered as to the cause, "just depends on which way the wind is blowin'."

I've discovered that my smarty-pants city ways of ripping off unsightly plastic and roofing material, has caused me a lot of trouble in the winter. I've also discovered that if the wind is blowing out of the southwest, I'd better let the faucets drip. You just never know.

My dad's childhood home (and mine for a brief time) was on a Scully lease southwest of Ramona. The house wasn't insulated and when the weather was dry the trim around the windows would shrink. "The snow would blow through the cracks around the window—fine as flour, and sift onto the inside window ledges, and not thaw," remembered Dad. Now that's cold!

"Dad would get up in the morning first thing and light a fire in the wood stove in the kitchen," said my father, reminiscing about Kansas winters. "He'd put the drinking water bucket on the stove to thaw. It would freeze solid during the night—indoors."

"We'd go out to milk and sometimes the milk in the pail would freeze before we got back to the house," my father continued. "We had to be so careful just going from the house to the barn, because you could lose your way with all the snow blowing in the air."

It's another day in the country, and I'm venturing outside. The snow squeaks under my boots and my mittens are warm and toasty as I walk down main street. The ice has transformed ordinary Ramona into a frosty fairy kingdom for a day.

As we walk down familiar sidewalks, past ancient trees, we pass the same buildings our ancestors did.
We're walking hand-in-hand with history. Circa 2001

Footprints in the Snow

In a small town, there aren't many footprints. When I stepped outside my front door this morning, mine were the first marks imprinted on the snow that covered the sidewalk.

Walking toward the office, I encountered Erich's footprints across my path heading toward his friend, Tony's, front door. It's his daily ritual to check on Tony first thing in the morning.

I felt like "The Tracker" as I continued down the main street, very much aware that my prints were the singular prints going south until a set of dog prints joined mine. The dog was evidently exploring in the early morning hours, and now my prints overlaid the paw marks.

There were diminutive bird tracks near a thawing puddle, and bunny hops across the sidewalk. There were prints I couldn't identify, and I turned back to check them out, chuckling at the fact that if someone else were tracking prints they would see that I'd turned around, and they would wonder what I was looking at—that thought, and its attendant smile, amused me until I reached the office door.

Early morning stillness. No cars going by. No one else visible. Just me, for now. Soon the community will be up and several sets of prints will be covering the sidewalk—my little friend Em will come in search of "something to do," my sister will be out on her exercise jaunt, Tony will walk down to get his mail. We'll all put our imprint on this winter morning as we've all put our imprint on this town.

When the first snow came one evening in December, I loved the fact that my car was the first to put tracks on the road as I drove toward home. There was no wind, just a thick blanket of white obliterating all the fallen leaves and potholes in my path. Snow outlined the dark tree limbs in the park and turned the weeds into magic wands.

Snow is a reminder of innocence. Snow invites us to an experience that is uncluttered, childlike, and refreshingly playful. For a little while, we can kick our feet in drifts of white that disintegrate like fluff, and in the process forget some of our concerns.

As transplants from California, seeing our first snow in many a year was so exciting that we got out a cheap plastic toboggan we'd found, hooked it up behind the car and went sliding around town at ten at night, trying to keep our squeals of delight to a minimum. You could see our skid marks all around the town and up and down the alleys as we searched for the softest snow.

When the snow came again this past week, we bundled up and went sledding again—after all, this may be our last big snowstorm of the season, and we just couldn't resist putting our print on its freshness, even though it was so cold we had to cover our faces to breathe.

Being so tied to the weather, life in the country offers lots of opportunities to start afresh. You don't have to wait through the four seasons with all their endings and beginnings to gain that sense of renewal. All it takes is snow.

As I watched the lazy snow flakes tumble from the sky week before last, I was reminded of the preciousness of life. Those fragile flakes were so heavy they splattered when they hit the window. It was like being inside a glass bauble that had just been turned upside down and then righted again.

My sister just walked into the office, "I knew you were here because I followed your footprints from the house," she laughed. "What on earth were you turning around for out there? To trick me?"

Jess told me it was comforting to see my footprints ahead of her. "I knew it was you," she said. "I could tell the print of your boots, and it was reassuring to know that you were blazing a trail."

Life seems so unpredictable for us city-dwellers here in the country, where it's snow today and mud tomorrow, impassable roads, and sidewalks that tilt at crazy angles.

On just another day in the country, even a walk to work becomes an adventure.

Our first winter in Ramona Tim got out an old car hood for us to go sledding on—this is Emily and Jess enjoying the ride. Circa 2001

Wanna Go Sledding?

Sledding is one of my favorite things to do. I'm not sure where this fascination came from—maybe my mother. On my twelfth Christmas—we were living in Kansas City—my parents presented me with my first sled—a red Flyer. It didn't get used much, because there weren't a lot of safe places for sledding in the big city.

After I was all grown up, living in Colorado, I fine-tuned my sledding ability. Living in Denver, we had trouble finding an unobstructed hill, free from traffic, and so we ended up sledding at the City Dump—there were lots of hills in that landfill.

And then we moved to Steamboat Springs, the snow capital of the world. We had very little money, certainly not enough to afford ski equipment or tow fees, so we went sledding on the red Flyer that I'd gotten for my twelfth birthday.

Nestled in the Yampa Valley, between mountain ranges, Steamboat Springs is an uphill, downhill kind of place and I was lucky enough to live on a country road that went downhill for two miles. Late at night—ensuring there was no traffic—we'd load our little sled onto our VW Bug, and drive uphill as far as we dared, get on the sled and ride down.

I'm not sure that I can adequately describe that sledding experience with moonlight flooding the white landscape, the night air still, cold, and crisp, without wind. High snow banks on both sides of the road made it like sledding down a tunnel. The only sounds that could be heard were the sled runners slicing through the frozen snow, and my exclamations of joy after executing particularly tricky corners. Pure undiluted pleasure.

Two miles flew by and before we knew it, we'd be at the main road—the highway that goes through Steamboat Springs—and we'd bail out into the ditch to stop our forward momentum. Now that was sledding!

In California, we went sledding on rare occasions, pulled by a horse. In Oregon, Dad would pull us out through the pasture, behind the tractor. Mom remembers going sledding as a youngster, living west of Ramona, on Ihde's Hill, or just sliding down a small hill out behind their farmhouse on a scoop shovel—they didn't have a sled at first, they improvised.

Warren Fike said he especially remembered sledding the winter of 1937 when the snow stayed on the ground for seven weekends. "Our Scout Master, Thurl Brehm, would tie a long tow rope behind his car and head out of town, picking up kids along the way. We could fasten our sleds in any free space along the rope. He'd end up with a dozen sleds behind him heading for Ihde's Hill."

"Going to Ihde Hill was like going to Estes Park for us kids. It was the closest thing to a mountain that we had out here on the prairie," said our mother.

We went sledding our first winter here—the Cheevers invited us to join their family fun—over by the Marion Reservoir. We climbed the steep banks up to the bridge, and then took a ten-second ride back down.

My biggest thrill, however, came from sledding around Ramona, late at night, behind Tim's truck. One year, we tried an old car hood—that was Tooltime Tim's childhood memory and his suggestion. Another year, we wore out two saucers—clean through to the gravel road, until the seat of our pants were scuffed. Finally, one year, we bought ourselves a two-man toboggan, which still survives.

You have to wait for the right conditions—late at night is best— when the snow is falling with big lazy flakes, and it piles up quickly on the already-frozen ground. The thrill is complete when there is snow-pack on the road and no car tracks.

Some years the snow is not deep enough or cold enough, or the wind is not calm enough. Some years, the roads are cleared before we have the heart to venture forth. This winter we did it in the early morning. It was lovely! After we'd exhausted ourselves, and the neighbor kids, I said to my 88-year-old mother, "You wanna go sledding?" She did!

After quite a ride around town, swearing I'd almost dumped her into the ditch by the park, I said. "Are you cold? You had enough?" She grinned and answered, "Well, maybe just a little more!" Now that was another day in the country to remember.

Don't they look angelic: Mikayla Antoszyk, Anna Weber, Andrea Kleiber. Bryanna Svoboda and in front is Kaitlin Brunner at the annual Festival of Lights Christmas Pageant—an event we created when we moved to town. Circa 2002

Make a Little Magic

When I tumbled out of bed this morning, there were at least two different ways to look at our living room. The house was either a mess with glue guns, bent hangers, scraps of tinsel and fabric all over the floor, *or* it was filled with Christmas Magic.

On the edge of the dining room table are fragile angel wings stacked up and ready for attachment to little angelic girls in Ramona for our town nativity. These exquisite wings were made from the hangers that came with Tooltime Tim's work uniforms, and he burned his finger twice on that glue gun as he helped make them.

On the mantle are two white stockings, hung with care. My daughter made them several years ago by hand—a Martha Stewart inspirational moment. They wait for Christmas morning, when they'll be stuffed with tiny gifts.

On the side table is Cousin Janet's magic star plate, with still a few Christmas goodies scattered between all the crumbs. There's a backdrop of little potted poinsettias—pink, not red—that graced Mom's birthday table earlier in the month, and snowmen candles with their black hats dripping and tipping.

This is indeed a house filled with magical memories of Christmas coming and Christmas past. There's a Cuckoo Clock on the wall that Doc bought for Emily, several years ago, in a fit of Christmas zeal. It has to be wound every day and he didn't even think about the fact that this chore would be too much for a little girl. So I told her that I'd keep the clock at my house until she's older and had a room of her own. Well, now she's old enough to receive it, and I must remember to wrap that clock.

The tiny tree on the little round table in front of the window is a small replica of the trees we used to decorate in California. The Ramona House is small so we can't drag in huge towering trees that touch the ceiling. Well, I shouldn't say we can't, because one Christmas we tried.

There are several packages in a corner that came in the mail, along with at least two, that still need to be mailed.

While my sister isn't Santa Clause, she's certainly one of his helpers and she has been making her list and checking it twice for at least a week.

Every evening Tim and I line up and ask, "What else needs to be checked off the list?" For some reason that list does not get smaller, it gets more detailed!

Over in the church, where Ramona's town Christmas event will be held this year, the manger awaits and the camel sits patiently in hopes that the wise men will soon appear. The shepherds give me daily reports as to whether or not we can have a live sheep indoors.

We're all waiting, looking forward, in anticipation of a little Christmas magic—like star-struck children in front of the Christmas tree.

Aunt Gertie's practicing the church organ while we make a stand for the Christmas star. Uncle Hank sings along in German as she plays *Silent Night* and we try to join in. Ah, how we savor the magical moments.

Mom calls and says, "Maybe Frieda's coming for Christmas!" with excitement in her voice, at the chance she may see her younger sister.

Magic is everywhere this time of year. You've got it at your house. It's hiding under the bed, stuffed away in a drawer, down deep in your heart, in the face of a loved one, the touch of a child, and in the very air we breathe. Once it happens, nothing can erase the mystical, magical memories.

It's what I've always wanted for Christmas, the *present*! And I've got it, because we're spending another day in the country with you!

A glimpse of The Ramona House at Christmas time. Our yearly goal is to get all the houses in Ramona with lights on them— an attainable goal since there are less than fifty homes in town. Circa 2002

Lighting Up the Prairie

We were returning to Ramona after spending Christmas in California. "Would all the Christmas lights in town still be on?"

We came around the corner by the railroad tracks and there they were—downtown was ablaze with Christmas cheer! Our five square blocks were a wonderful sight to behold.

There's a unique quality to Christmas lights on the prairie where the night is pitch-black, and streets lamps are few and far between. Those cheerful multicolored strands stand out like jewels on the dark, winter landscape. The all-white twinkling lights rival the stars for beauty and sparkle like diamonds.

Uncle Hank tells me that when he was a boy there was no such thing as Christmas lights decorating the houses or the trees. Electricity had not come to rural Kansas. There was Christmas excitement, though.

On Christmas eve, the family was bundled up for the ride to the church for services. One year they had a big snow, and the roads were drifted shut so John Lorei, who worked for the Schubert family and later married one of their daughters, got out the lumber wagon and hitched up the horses and drove the family four and one-half miles across the pastures to St. Paul Lutheran church, which stood for many years northeast of Ramona.

Grandma heated bricks and wrapped them in newspaper, and put them in the straw on the bottom of the wagon. Dressed in their Sunday best—along with long underwear, coats, gloves, and hats—and covered with blankets, the children endured the long bumpy ride with relative ease.

At the church, the children all got a surprise after the program. "Usually it was an orange and some nuts and a few pieces of candy. We thought it was great," says Uncle Hank.

As a finale to the service, the candles were lit on the Christmas tree and everyone gathered around to sing, *O Tannenbaum, O Tannenbaum wie treu sind deine Blätter*, in German.

"I'll never forget those trustees walking around that blazing tree. They had big long poles that had a wet rag tied to the end so they could put out any fire that might start from those candles," Hank remembers. "It's a wonder we didn't burn that church down."

After the glory of seeing the candles on the Christmas tree and getting goodies, it was time for the ride home. This time, four and one-half miles seemed much longer. "The ground was frozen and that wagon had no springs," Hank laughs at the memory. "The bricks were cold and we were about frozen when we finally got home."

Their mother would be the first in the house, to light the lamp—and there, like magic, was another Christmas tree with presents underneath—another Christmas Glory!

All through the week between Christmas and New Year's, the family Christmas tree remained in the parlor, and then on New Year's eve, the candles were brought out and placed on their tree and nine little children stood in awe, their faces bathed in candlelight as another year melted into history, and a new year began.

Ninety-eight Christmases for my Aunt Anna, ninety-one for Uncle Hank, sixty-seven for me, and each year I seek the thrill of Christmas on a dark winter night. I've searched for it from New York to Delhi, from California to Kansas, in big crowds of strangers or with family gathered around, and I find it most sweetly in the still of the night, where stars shine bright, in the country.

Two old lawn chairs, given to us by Aunt Gertie, stand in the wintertime yard, symbolic of two sisters
who came from California to live in Kansas. Circa 2001

Winter Wondering

From the other room I hear a voice intoning, "As the sun warms the earth, so morning yoga warms the body-mind."

My sister is up and doing yoga. I should go join her, but I'm a little reticent. While the yoga instructor on the video tape reclines on a warm Hawaiian beach in the glow of early morning sunrise, at the moment Jessica's bottom meditates on a drafty ice-cold floor. Now that takes true grit!

To be honest, living in the country has taken some getting used to. There are some big considerations, such as the pay scale—it's challenging to make a living. There are silly little inconveniences—like yesterday when I went to the grocery store and attempted to find Cambazola cheese. No one had heard of it. Suddenly, my very soul hungered for French bread, baked daily and delivered warm from the bakery, slathered with rich Cambazola.

As I start the Kansas winter ritual of lighting the fire in the wood stove, I tease myself with thoughts of the California rituals.

"Wouldn't it be lovely," I mumble into my cup of instant coffee, "to be sitting on a terrace in the middle of a warm, sun-drenched, winter day at the Napa Valley Roasting Company, choosing from ten different kinds of brewed coffee and eating pastries with elegant names?"

"Wouldn't it be nice," I mutter as I peer into the refrigerator at a head of lettuce which was irretrievably wilted in the shipping process, "to be sitting in my favorite Napa Valley restaurant, waiting for one of their choice salads with an unpronounceable name?"

"Wouldn't it be great," I muse remembering the days when my winter wardrobe was tailored suits instead of survival sweats, "to wear boots as a fashion statement and not a necessity?"

I do this kind of winter wondering to test my country living resolve.

I wonder if I'll ever want to exchange this place, this pace, for some other kind of adventure, or something easier and warmer?

I wonder if life in the country will ever become boring, hum-drum, and too normal? At what point will I cease to be filled with wonder at this venture we've undertaken?

These are definitely winter wonderings as my coffee rapidly chills, and I sit in solitude at the kitchen table.

A train whistles in the distance and calls out its impending arrival at the crossing. Any minute now, I'll hear Tooltime Tim's old truck heading this way—he's volunteered to help me organize the tool shed today.

The train calls again. "Tim had better hurry or he'll be stuck on the other side of the tracks." I think to myself.

Silence fills the house. It's so quiet I can hear the clock ticking. And then it hits me. "This is it!" I say right out loud.

I'm not here in the country because of the money, the food or the convenience. The simplicity of existence is why we're here—where you know your neighbors, where your soul is soothed when you hear meadowlarks sing, where you feel safe enough to leave your doors open and a traffic jam is two parked cars and a dog in the road.

Our return to the country has been a good move. We'll just bake our own French bread, create our own exotic salads, and I'll settle for longhorn cheese instead of Cambazola.

Come to think of it, I haven't really lost much coming back to Kansas, except for sound pollution, traffic jams, and exotic prices which I'll gladly trade for another day in the country.

Index